By Way of Introduction ...

From out of Detroit's diverse neighborhoods and network of city streets have emerged some of the world's greatest writers, musicians, entrepreneurs, thinkers, athletes and personalities. This book contains their stories. Not their biographies, but rather personal anecdotes reflecting on memorable moments from time spent in or around Detroit — a fascinating glimpse into each of their lives and experiences, many of which you might also share. So many legendary people have passed through Detroit that to include each and every person's contribution would have been an impossible task, so this book brings you individuals who come from a wide range of disciplines to create the unique fabric of our city. Some of them you will instantly recognize. Some you may not. Some were born here. Others moved here to build their lives and careers. Just like our river, our music, our cars, our industry, our struggles and our triumphs, these men and women have shaped our city and, in many ways, the culture of our nation and our world. Enjoy a conversation with each of them.

The Ambassador Bridge | *Tunnel to Canada*

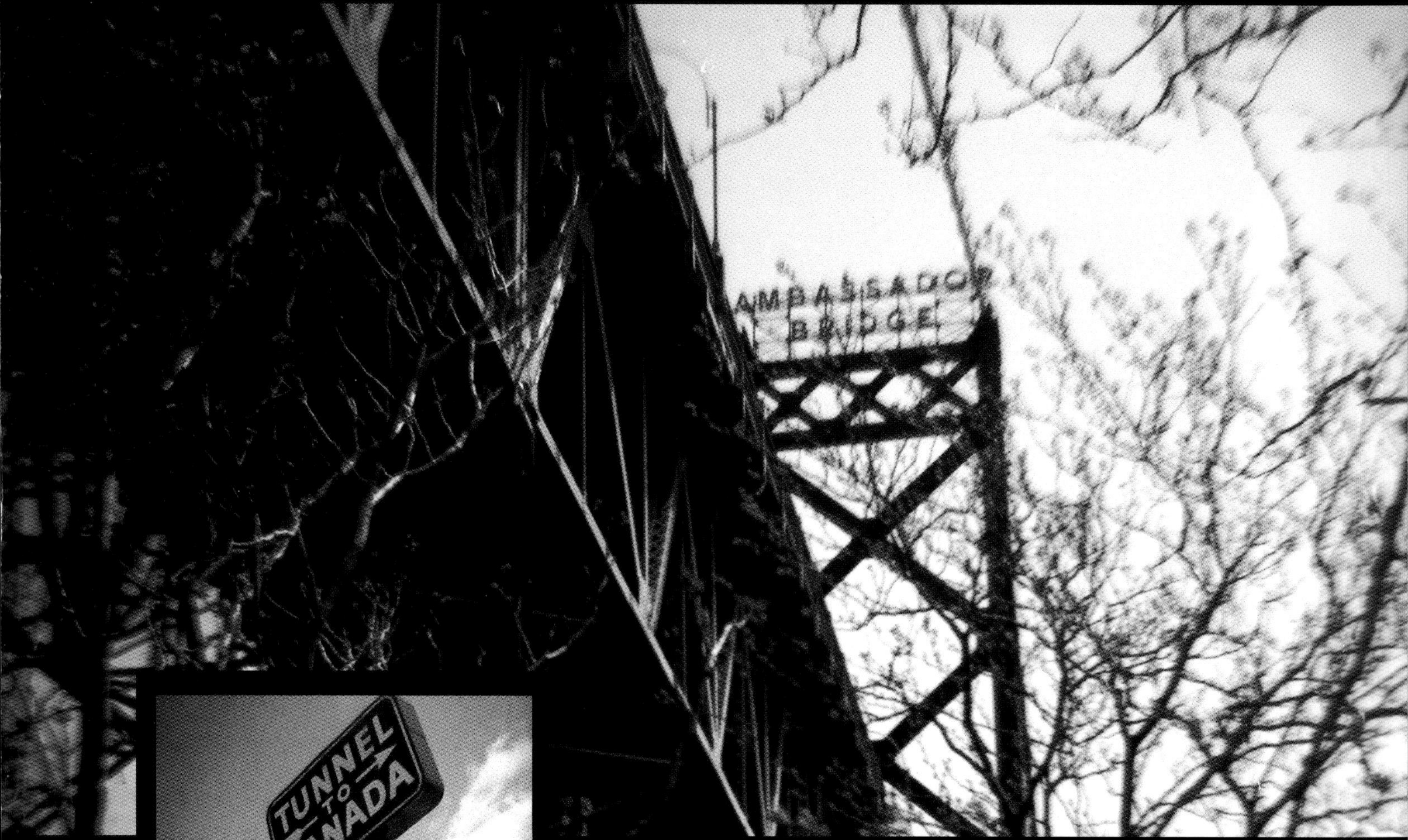

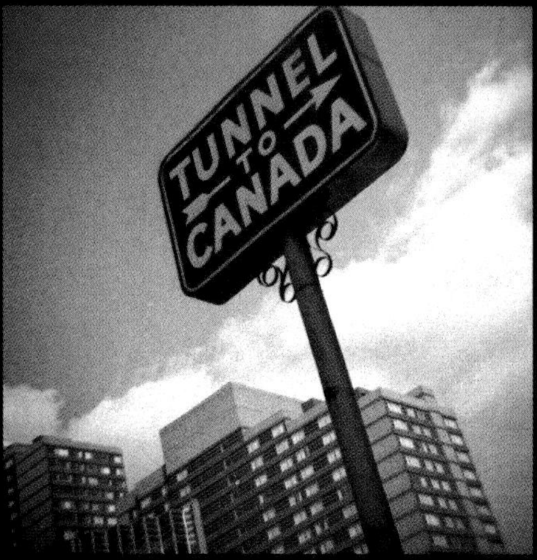

Dedicated to ...
Jackie, Alex, Sal, Victoria, Chris, Ashton and Bill

In Celebration ...
We would like to acknowledge the lives, spirit and contributions of three great Detroiters,
Betty Carter, Marshall Fredericks and Ann Mikolowski, who passed away during the making of this book.
Through their legacies, generations of future Detroiters will find inspiration and hope.

TABLE OF CONTENTS

TABLE OF CONTENTS

FOREWORD
Tim Kiska

Detroit has always had a hard time patting itself on the back.

About 20 years ago, a young businesswoman by the name of Emily Gail came up with the slogan: "Say Nice Things About Detroit." Lots of people snickered about that one. Most insisted she was whistling by the intensive care ward, since it was plain to see that the city's main arteries — Grand River, Jefferson, Gratiot, Michigan Avenue — were in a bad way. Others cynically believed she was an opportunist who thought up the catchy slogan for publicity. But "say nice things about Detroit?" Ha! What kind of naive idiot would come up with something like that? What an absurd proposition!

Fact is, we've always given ourselves credit for making fine automobiles. We may be the best metal-benders in the world. But we've never given ourselves credit for the fine roster of writers, sculptors, journalists, entrepreneurs, actors and actresses we've produced. Even when the rest of the country looks at our creative output with awe.

Which is the wonder of this book. It catalogs some of the town's greatest creators, and lets them tell their stories in their own words.

When you look at the list between these two covers, we have nothing to feel bad about. Let's talk about writers. We've got Elmore Leonard. Sculptors? We had Marshall Fredericks, who is as fine a gentleman and artist as ever walked the earth. Love him or hate him, Bill Bonds was as effective an anchorman as anybody in this country. Actors and actresses? How about Julie Harris, Jeff Daniels, Lily Tomlin, and Selma Blair? We've got Shirley Muldowney. Great athletes such as Al Kaline, Gordie Howe, and boxing manager Emanuel Steward.

Somehow, there is something about the city psyche that forbids braggadocio. It's like we're flying too close to the sun if we actually admit that the city is actually an artistic center. And what we're really good at is ripping people down. Eminem, the Detroit-based rap star, sold more records in one week during Spring, 2000 than any other artist in the world. But he and his wife get busted partying at a bar in Warren, so the Monday morning water cooler conversation is the arrest — not the fact that a guy who was slinging burgers only three years ago was a top recording star.

And what we're really good at is knocking ourselves. Wasn't this the town that had two of the worst riots in U.S. history? And, oh yeah. Some guy named Bubba had his picture taken in front of a flaming cop car after the 1984 World Series. Are we a bunch of sweethearts, or what?

FOREWORD

And we get defensive. Way too defensive. When ABC's Judd Rose came to town and pointed out some rather obvious problems on *PrimeTime Live*, we acted hurt. The mayor cussed him out, the morning talk show hosts and newspapers wouldn't stop talking about it, and we acted as if we'd all gotten a failing grade on our report card. In Chicago or New York, the reaction would have been, "Yeah? What's your point?"

Maybe we wouldn't be so defensive if we started recognizing the talent that lives here. This book would be a terrific starting point for that. Yes, Detroit is an honest, hard-working, lunch bucket town that loves sports (particularly bowling), potato chips and talks tough. And that's great. We should be proud of that. But it's also the home of Ted Nugent and Sue Marx, and the place where Wyland and Christine Lahti first began practicing their craft. One doesn't diminish the other. These people aren't the exceptions to the rule. They are the rule. This is the home of great talent, and this book celebrates that fact.

Forget Cleveland. Forget Pittsburgh. For the moment, their downtowns may be better than ours. But so what. The people in the book are some of the most creative and accomplished in the world. And they live here.

Look at it another way: oysters are just oysters until they are irritated by grit and/or dirt. Then, they produce pearls. This town has plenty of grit. So it has plenty of pearls. This is a partial collection of the town's pearls.

So say nice things about Detroit.

Monument To Joe Louis

The City of Detroit, fondly referred to as "Motown," has a rich and brilliant history filled with the sounds of the automobiles and music that have been created here. Around every corner you will find a great story — stories of people and places that make up the fabric of our city.

Every Detroiter can relate a story of shared experiences ... a chance meeting at Lafayette Coney Island, hearing a performance at Baker's Keyboard Lounge or Soup Kitchen Saloon, or watching fireworks soar high above the Detroit River.

We are a city that is proud of its past, but looking forward to its future. This book is a fine collection of extraordinary stories focusing on people from our past and present who embody what this city is all about. All Detroiters will appreciate the tales they tell, and will remember stories of their own while reading them.

Dennis W. Archer

Dennis W. Archer
Mayor of Detroit

The Uniroyal Tire

motor city memoirs

THE PEOPLE AND THEIR STORIES

Wyland is a painter, sculptor, muralist and writer.
Photographed while painting his mural on the side of the David Broderick Tower in Detroit.

At the age of 16, I was working night and day in our basement on my drawing, on my painting, on my sculpture, on everything until I put together an incredible portfolio. One evening my mom came in and showed me an article that had appeared in *The Detroit News* about a famous airbrush artist named Shrunken Head. Considered by many to be one of the best airbrush artists in the world, his real name was Dennis Poosch. He lived in Detroit where he was doing quite well air-brushing fantastic murals on vans. I guess what caught my mother's eye in the article was that Shrunken Head had a great interest in Salvador Dali, who she knew was my favorite artist.

"Why don't you go down and see this guy, and see if he'll hire you?" she asked. I put together my portfolio, found his studio and went up and pounded on his door. Now this was no ordinary door; it was a psychedelic purple with a small head in the middle of it that looked like a wrinkled-up apple. It looked like a shrunken head, but it was probably plastic. It had long, black straggly hair and a bone through its nose.

Suddenly the purple door swung open, and there stood a larger living replica of the creepy little door ornament. It was him, Shrunken Head. Only, instead of being some kind of pagan cannibal, he was just a very friendly hippie, and very cool.

The studio was huge. There were outrageous murals and canvases everywhere. A set of stairs led down to a cavernous floor where at least 20 custom vans sat with their sides, backs and front ends covered with brilliant murals in various stages of completion. This was a big, big operation; two Doberman pinschers were loping around the joint, stopping every now and then to sniff me and let me know they ran the place.

We sat down and looked through my book, and after a few minutes Shrunken Head said, "So, you're into Dali?"

"Yeah," I replied.

"Me, too. This work is incredible. You're very talented. Have you ever done any airbrush?"

"Not really," I told him. "But I think I can do it."

He led me downstairs where he was halfway done with a van. He started painting, and I settled in behind him to watch.

"You think you can do this?" he asked, handing me the gun. Without answering, I took it and sat down. "Finish it," he said.

To my great amazement, he left and didn't come back for several hours. I mean, here was a $4,000 custom mural, and he just handed it to me. I could have destroyed the whole thing. It was like learning to swim; he just threw me into the water. I made a hundred mistakes, dripping paint all over the place. But, in each place I dripped, I transformed the mistake into a rock, which has since become sort of a trademark for me.

Dennis came back a few hours later and viewed my work. To make a long story short, he hired me on the spot, and I worked under his tutelage for four months. This is where I learned how to use all kinds of spray guns, including the larger ones for putting in background colors. We did all the big auto shows in Detroit, painting murals on the sides of vans, drawing large audiences to watch us work. This, I guess, is where I first started painting in public, an invaluable learning experience that has served me extremely well on my Whaling Wall project.

Working for Dennis Poosch was a groundbreaker for me. Shrunken Head Studios was my first job in my chosen profession, and I'll be forever in this man's debt. In addition to training me in all the tools of the trade, he showed me that I, too, could go out and do it. I could be a working artist, doing exactly what I loved to do. He was a great mentor for me, and I worked 12-hour shifts for him without even thinking about it. In fact, I often spent the night at the studio, working all day and all night.

Prior to focusing on my art full time, I spent three days working in Detroit factories. As I look back, I now realize that my short career in the factories was really a godsend. I can be a very spiritual person, and I firmly believe I was sent to those jobs so I could learn how to appreciate the talent I had and develop it. Ironically, the experience taught me about work ethic. I bore down tirelessly on my artwork and haven't stopped since.

"

I can be a very spiritual person,

and I firmly believe I was sent to those jobs

so I could learn how to appreciate the

talent I had and develop it.

"

Julie Harris is an actress.
Photographed on Broadway, New York City, New York.

My father and mother both loved the theater very, very much, so I guess it's not surprising that I made it my career. When we were growing up they would take my brothers and me to touring companies coming through Detroit; it was a natural thing for me to love theater because they did, too. They talked about plays and actors and directors all the time at home, and they would go to see plays and tell us about them. I was the middle child; I had an older brother, Bill, who was a year older than I and a younger brother, Richard, who was five years younger, and all three of us benefited from my parents' love of theater.

I remember my parents took us to the Cass Theatre and the Schubert — I don't think either of them exists anymore. The Cass Theatre was wonderful, and I used to see plays from the top balcony, which was far away from the stage. We saw some truly memorable performances ... I remember seeing the uncut version of *Hamlet,* done by Maurice Evans, an English actor ... we saw a very moving play called *Native Son* directed by Orson Welles ... and I saw Ethel Waters (my darling of the waters) in *Cabin in the Sky,* a musical and a drama, and I fell in love with my Ethel Waters then. She was a wonderful performer.

We all loved going to movies, too. So much so that my brothers and I would see the films, then re-enact them when we came home. We would recreate them in the house or outside on the lawn — we lived on Windmill Pointe Drive in Grosse Pointe. We had a big lawn, and alongside it, between our house and the Morans' was a little wooded area, and we used to act out the scenes in those woods, which was perfect after we'd seen *Tarzan,* for swinging from the trees and all that. *Tarzan* was serialized, so we saw many of those films, with Johnny Weismuller and Maureen O'Sullivan. We also saw *Rin Tin Tin,* and the Andy Hardy movies with Mickey Rooney — I loved Mickey Rooney. I think he was the greatest Puck in the world in *Midsummer Night's Dream.*

I went away to school when I was in my junior year in high school, but before that I went to Grosse Pointe Country Day, which was a beautiful school. It was a nice structure, well-run, it was a fun place to learn, and the teachers were wonderful. You started in kindergarten and you graduated from the same school, which was a great way to grow and make lasting friendships. I have many friends I made in my school years that I still see today. My childhood in Detroit was a wonderful combination of friends, family and theater — a great place to grow up.

Emanuel Steward is a Hall of Fame boxing trainer and manager.
Photographed at the Kronk gym in Detroit.

I cried all the way to Detroit. It was 1956, and I was 11 years old and living in West Virginia when my parents separated. On a Friday night, I left with my mom on a train for Detroit. I'll never forget that trip; it was raining and I cried the whole way looking out the window. We got here on a Saturday night and stayed with my aunt. She lived on the east side, right at Holcomb and Mack.

On Sunday morning, I got up and went outside for the first time in the city. I got in a fight within about 10 minutes, with a boy who I found out later was one of the tough guys. I was talking with my cousin who had just come by to see me, and this kid was out there. I said, "Look at that boy across the road there." And he said, "Road? That's a street. We don't say road here." Then he started making fun of the way I talked. Right away I tripped him and we started fighting right there on the sidewalk. My aunt said, "Oh, boy, I've got a problem here."

The second week in school, I got in a fight with a guy who had just broken out of the juvenile detention. They were looking for him. He heard that I was liking his girlfriend, and he had broken out of school for that. He was about 15 years old; much older than we were, and he was like a real gangster guy everybody was afraid of. When he came on the school playground after school was out, everybody started running away — but I didn't know what was going on. I beat him, they stopped us, and we started fighting again and I beat him up again. Finally after that he quit, and suddenly I had a reputation.

I had a dual personality. In school, I was very quiet, always on the honor roll, but once I left school, I had a whole different world. There was a bunch of guys I got with, and all we'd do was go around to different blocks fighting all the time. One time the police brought me home and told my mother that the next time they locked me up I was going

to go to juvenile school. So she decided to take me back to a boxing gym — I had been boxing since I was eight, but I had stopped when the CYO closed. She took me to a place called the Brewster Center, through Detroit Parks and Recreation. Joe Louis and Sugar Ray Robinson had trained there. I won the city's junior championship for kids from 10 to 15 at 110 pounds in 1959. The next year I picked up 10 pounds, came back and won it again. It changed my whole life. I got really serious into my boxing then, and I got out of most of my street fighting — not all of it — in the evenings, which we were still doing a lot of. That's why I think sports is so great for kids. All of a sudden I was reading my name all over the papers, I was in study hall in school in the morning and the teachers would say, we've got a special student, one of your classmates just won the championship, he was in *The Detroit News.*

In 1962, I went to Chicago for the national Golden Gloves championship. We stayed at a place called the Conrad Hilton Hotel — I had never stayed at a hotel in my life. I couldn't believe that someone came in and made up your bed for you, and I couldn't believe we had a paper they brought every day free, *The Wall Street Journal.* We went to eat in a restaurant, and they asked me, "How do you want your steak?" I didn't know; the only kind of steak I knew was what my mama used to beat with a hammer. So a couple of the guys I was with, Bill O'Brien and Chuck Fecay, rather than have me embarrassed, said, "Give him a sirloin steak." The next morning we had breakfast, same thing. They said, "How do you want your egg? Do you want it poached? Sunny-side up?" That's when I began to realize that there was a different life beyond the life that I had lived. All my life being raised in for the most part ghetto-type neighborhoods you never know that. That week I lost the first fight of my life. I lost to the guy who went on to win the national championship. I stayed and I watched him win in the finals of the program. I was ashamed to have lost the fight. I was so embarrassed and humiliated, not realizing at that time you had 58 champions come in from 58 cities — it was called the Tournament of Champions — that was where all the best fighters come. And naturally, those guys were much older and more experienced, and I guess I should have lost. But I was upset and embarrassed. People said later that the hardest fight the championship winner had in the tournament was with the tall kid from Detroit, the first fight of the tournament. He ended up knocking everybody else out, virtually.

I went home totally obsessed with winning that gold glove with the diamond. I said, "I'm winning that thing next year." They said, "Man, no Detroiter's won." I said, "I'm winning it." Winning and losing in life is in the mind of the individual. When I came back home, I really started to pick it up in boxing and school. I came back the next year, and I beat the guy who had beaten me and went on to win the national Golden Gloves championship. When I got home I got a nice letter from the mayor, Jerome Cavanagh, congratulating me and thanking me. The whole city had a little parade; it was such a good feeling. Today that's what I'm most proud of. I still can look back in *The World Almanac* and tell my kids, "See in 1963, your daddy was the number-one Golden Gloves boxer in America."

People in Detroit have been very supportive of me from the time I was a little junior boxer, through when I was a Golden Gloves fighter, through when I started promoting and managing fighters like Tommy Hearns and Mickey Goodwin. The city came out and supported us. The crowds would come out to support boxing. I've had a tremendous amount of success and support from the city. That's why I could never leave Detroit. And wherever I go, I can't wait to get home to Detroit. I love my neighborhood in Rosedale Park; there's nothing more beautiful on a morning like today than to get up, go for a jog in the park, meet and talk with people. Having been a native Detroiter, I'm running across people when I go to the store, saying, "How are you doing, Mr. Steward . . . how's your daughter doing . . . I used to know your mother . . ." Just different things that you really miss, being away from home.

I travel all over the world — Germany, Italy, Australia, Norway, England, Mexico — and I'm always anxious to get to Detroit. People say, "You want to get back to that raggedy city?" I say, "The fight's going to be over on a Friday night; at Saturday, 7 or 8 in the morning, I'm gone." I've packed all of the equipment that we needed over the eight weeks or however long I had to be there, all those trunks with everything all packed up, sent it off to Detroit and I am gone. They say, "What are you doing?" I say, "I'm going home." They ask me why, and I say, "I just want to be at home in the morning." And I love going down to the Kronk gym; it's got so many memories there, 30 years of them now. I can still picture Tommy Hearns when he was just a skinny kid there.

On holidays, you just ride around the city, you smell barbecue all over, you stop from one house to the other and people are drinking beer and playing cards and there's music playing all over. It's something that, unless you were raised in Detroit, you would never understand. It's a feeling, it's a part of me, and when I'm sitting in other places I get homesick, and I want to go home.

"

I went home totally obsessed with winning that gold glove

with the diamond. I said, 'I'm winning that thing next year.'

They said, 'Man, no Detroiter's won.'

I said, 'I'm winning it.'

"

Mort Crim is a broadcast journalist and pilot.
Photographed aboard his airplane at City Airport in Detroit.

Most people I know want to live as far away from the airport as possible.

Not me. I want to live as close as possible. I'd probably live *at* the airport if I could. I'm sure that, sometimes, my wife thinks I do.

Flying has always been an important part of my life, and during the two decades we've lived in the Detroit area, it's been a central part. While it began as a hobby when I was in high school — before I was old enough to drive a car — by the time we arrived in Michigan, flying had become a significant part of my career.

During my years as a TV anchor and reporter, we used my plane often to crisscross the state of Michigan — covering the infamous prison riots in the early '80s, researching and reporting a series of stories on pollution and putting ourselves at the right spot for dozens of breaking stories. There were more trips than I can count to Lansing, Kalamazoo and Mackinac Island — as well as frequent flights to Chicago, New York and Washington. Terry Oprea, one of the most talented people in television — and now president of Mort Crim Communications, Inc. — frequently accompanied me on these trips as producer and unofficial co-pilot.

Occasionally Terry would ask, "What do I do with this thing if you ever keel over at the controls?" I assured him that flying an airplane is easier that producing a TV show. Fortunately, we never had to test the theory.

One of the most memorable flights involved a visit to Flint by President Jimmy Carter. He was scheduled to deliver a speech at the airport at 3 p.m. Ah, perfect: I would fly a producer, photographer and myself to Flint, cover the president's address and news conference, fly back to City Airport and have the video edited in plenty of time for the 5 o'clock news.

There was only one hitch which we hadn't considered. At the end of the president's visit, the Flint airport was closed to all outgoing and incoming traffic until Air Force One had departed with the president. The three of us sat nervously in our plane for what seemed like hours, waiting — not patiently — for clearance to take off.

Instead of arriving back at City Airport by 4 or 4:15 as we had planned, our wheels touched down at 4:35. We had exactly 25 minutes before I was due on the air, and we would be encountering evening rush hour traffic between City Airport and our studios on West Lafayette Boulevard.

At five minutes before 5, I shot through the station's back door, the producer right behind me — videotape in hand. Someone from the newsroom held the door open as I rushed into the green room, ran a comb quickly through my hair — no time for TV make-up this time — and made a mad dash for the studio. I slipped into my seat beside co-anchor Carmen Harlan just two minutes before the red light came on and it was time to say, "Good evening . . ."

Now that I've left the anchor desk and am broadcasting *Second Thoughts* daily on more then 700 radio stations, the airplane has become an increasingly significant transportation tool. During one 20-month period, I was in more then 100 cities. All but five of those trips were made in my airplane. The aircraft makes it possible for me to attend board meetings, conferences, book signings and dozens of other events that simply couldn't be accommodated using commercial airlines. I can — and do — land at small, out-of-the-way airports the large jets don't serve.

Despite its practical applications, flying has never stopped being fun. There's a strong bond that develops between pilots. When I first arrived in Detroit back in August, 1978, Sonny Eliot was a co-owner of the restaurant at Detroit City Airport. It was called "Sonny's Weather Station" and it was a major hangout for corporate and private pilots. I spent many a Saturday afternoon sipping coffee with Sonny and the other assorted flyers — especially on those days when Michigan's weather turned sour. While Sonny and I enjoyed working together at WDIV-TV, we shared even greater times at the airport.

Many of my closest friendships since moving to Detroit revolve around airplanes. Some started because of a mutual love of flying. Dr. John Burrows, Dr. Richard Mertz, Chuck Gaidica, Bob Shafer, Robert and Alice Gustafson, Phil Foster and, of course, the incorrigible Sonny Eliot.

We will always be Detroiters. But, Renee and I are reaching a point in our lives when we want to spend more of the cold winter months in Florida. So, recently, we purchased a home on Amelia Island. A friend asked me, "Why Amelia?"

Let's see — by my stopwatch, our house is exactly four minutes from the airport.

Any more questions?

"

Many of my closest

friendships since moving to Detroit

revolve around airplanes.

"

Mitch Ryder is a musician.
Photographed at Alvin's in Detroit.

Another bitter cold winter was fast approaching the Detroit area. A man was hurriedly preparing his home when there was a desperate knock on the door. He opened the door and saw nothing. As he went to close the door he glanced at the porch and saw a tiny snail. The snail looked up at the man and said, "Oh, mister, it's going to be so very cold this winter … could I please stay with you in your nice, warm house?" The man paused for a moment and drew back his foot and quickly kicked the little snail hundreds of yards away.

Three years later … a knock at the door. The man opens the door and the little snail, driven by indignation, screams out, "What's up with that?"

Somewhere in the Detroit area, a family sits down at the table for dinner. At the head of the table sits the Grandfather. He leans over to touch the son and he passes gas. Thousands of miles away, in the foothills of the Andes Mountains, a lowly peasant farmer leans over to pet his pig. Coincidence? I think not.

The dogged persistence with which we approach our struggles in this region is a testament to the strength of our will. Our sense of self is well balanced enough to afford us our dignity. The mysteries of life do not astound us. We lay comfortably somewhere near the top of the food chain.

I was asked to write some favorite memories of growing up and living in Detroit and the near. There are simply too many. Good and bad. I would rather just tell you that I wouldn't trade them for anything in the world.

Adam Cardinal Maida is Archbishop of Detroit.
Photographed at the Nevada Campus of Cornerstone Schools in Detroit.

THE CORNERSTONE SEED

When sown upon the ground, the mustard seed is the smallest of all seeds, but when it has grown it is the greatest of all the bushes and becomes a tree, so that the birds of the air come and make nests in its branches.

— Gospel of Matthew

It was more than a speech, it was a *seed.* When I addressed the Economic Club of Detroit in October of 1990, I proposed a partnership — a partnership with business, civic and religious leaders to provide a new educational opportunity for the children within the urban community of Detroit. That proposal quickly germinated and took root. In fact, I have come to believe this singular idea has helped to cultivate the local educational landscape in a most remarkable way.

Cornerstone Schools opened in August of 1991 and, like the mustard seed, have thrived. The third millennium will witness the 500th graduate from Cornerstone Schools.

The "design phase" of Cornerstone Schools came during my first year as Archbishop of Detroit. It was an enlightening and encouraging introduction to how this diverse community — city and suburban — can pull together and get things done.

The initial coalition which formulated plans for the pre-kindergarten through eighth grade Cornerstone Schools included Baptist, Episcopalian, Lutheran and Roman Catholic leaders. I recall how, together with civic and business leaders, we committed ourselves to making Cornerstone Schools "centers of hope" for inner-city children and their families. While classes in religious doctrine would not be required, an essential part of the year-round program *would* include instruction in Christian values and moral decision making. Tuition would be set, but no student would be turned away for lack of funds. Within a matter of months, corporate sponsors stepped up to defray educational costs for each and every student. Besides giving money, the business partners also agreed to serve as mentors. At the same time, each parent or guardian was asked to sign a "covenant," an agreement to become actively involved in the Cornerstone program.

In my Economic Club address, I offered a challenge "to think in a new way ... to break out of our old molds and categories." Reaction from the news media was swift and favorable. "A major educational asset" was the way one local paper described our plan for Cornerstone Schools. "We have few doubts that good teachers and administrators would want to work at such schools and that parents would stand in long lines to enroll their children there."

In the years that followed, as the Cornerstone seed sprouted and grew, I watched with great hope as more seeds — more new ideas — were planted in the fields of education. In 1993, to deal with at-risk, teenage boys, many performing at sixth or seventh grade levels, an innovative high school was established in the core city by the Archdiocese of Detroit and the Jesuits: Loyola Academy.

Responding to yet another educational concern, corporations and business leaders, from here and afar, again impressed me with their creativity and generosity in developing two scholarship programs to meet the needs of inner-city students and their parents. As a result, parochial school students in Detroit, nearly 70 percent of them non-Catholic, soon became the recipients of millions of scholarship dollars distributed by the Pathways of Hope Foundation and Pathways PLUS. Even the public sector unveiled new school funding proposals. As for Cornerstone Schools, the opinion writers were correct; in no time, the waiting lists filled with more names than the total enrollment.

Several years ago at an awards ceremony in Washington, DC, a Cornerstone eighth grader told his story: "I worked harder in the first week at Cornerstone than I had worked the whole year at my other school. I managed to get out of a gang and make my life straight. After high school, I will go on to college to get a degree in veterinary medicine."

Those words affirm my heartfelt belief that *every* child deserves access to an education that nurtures human potential. The Cornerstone motto was well-chosen: "Preparing Children for Life."

My fondest memory of Detroit will be forever sown with the parable of the mustard seed.

If you have faith the size of a mustard seed, *nothing will be impossible for you.*

"

My fondest memory of Detroit will be forever sown

with the parable of the mustard seed.

If you have faith the size of a mustard seed,

nothing will be impossible for you.

Sue Marx is a filmmaker.
Photographed in the Detroit Film Theatre at the Detroit Institute of Arts in Detroit.

They told us to be brief. We were warned that, if we won, we'd have a total of 60 seconds in which to say all of our thank-yous. After that, they said the orchestra would "play us off the stage." And, as if we weren't nervous enough, they also reminded us that the Academy Awards were being watched by one-and-a-half billion people worldwide. Five nominations in our category, a 20 percent chance to win an Oscar and 60 seconds in which to remember to thank everyone who worked on *Young at Heart*. And to thank Reva and Lou, the octogenarian stars of the documentary who were seated in the audience with us. And to thank husbands, boyfriends, the usual. I'm a long-time Detroit resident and, if given the chance, I was determined to use some of my precious 30 seconds to let the Hollywood crowd know that they're not the only ones who can make movies. In addition to my thank-yous, I planned to say something short like "Hooray for Michigan." Same three syllables — Holl-y-wood. Mich-i-gan. Finally, the Short Documentary category. The presenters reeled off the names of all five contenders and their films. Then we heard, "And the winner is … " and, in what's best described as an out-of-body experience, we floated up to the stage to claim our Oscars. We each said our thank-yous, and quaking and shaking and holding my eight-and-a-half-pound Oscar up in the air, I shouted, "From Hollywood … Hooray for Michigan!" That line made the front page of the Detroit newspapers the next day. It also made Mayor Coleman Young mad as hell. "Why didn't you say, 'Hooray for Detroit?'" he growled when I saw him a week or so later. "De-troit, Mr. Mayor, has only two syllables. It needed three — like Hollywood." A little later, I figured it out. He always called it "De-troy-et." I guess that's why Governor Blanchard gave a big party in our honor at the governor's mansion … and why the mayor of my city, whom I dearly loved and for whom I had produced films and campaign spots, only sent a note. My belated apologies, Coleman. We miss you.

Jerry Uelsmann is a photographer, author and graduate professor emeritus at the University of Florida.

Photographed at his home in Gainesville, Florida.

I grew up in Detroit on LaSalle, near Fenkell. It was a very user-friendly area at that time. We were within walking distance of the shops on Livernois, and as kids we would walk to a lot of different theaters, like the Avalon and the Picadilly or, if we were feeling ambitious, we would ride our bikes over to Highland Park, which was a great place to explore. It was a nice world. My dad had an independent grocery store at Forest and Trumbull; his father owned it before him. So I started working at an early age, I'd say around third grade, after school. I had a wagon that I'd use to deliver groceries. In those days, grocery stores were nothing like the ones you see today. People would call up and say they needed a dozen eggs, or some potatoes or whatever, and I'd deliver them. Outside of school and work, my mom always tried to do nice things for us. She made me take piano lessons once, which I hated. My brother survived that, I think. But I had always done a bit of drawing, so one time my mom found out there was a class in charcoal drawing offered at the Detroit Institute of Arts. It was convenient, because it wasn't too far from my dad's store. Suddenly I was introduced to this great museum. And I remember very clearly a Van Gogh self-portrait that they owned there. I didn't know who Van Gogh was, but I was intensely interested in this portrait. It was vibrant, glowing. It was an unusual encounter for me, coming from a nice family, but one that had little knowledge of the world of art.

I developed an interest in photography over time. My dad did photography as a hobby. Initially my brother got interested, and I got dragged along to the camera store. And back then I hated it, I must say. I wondered, "What is this? What am I doing here?" It wasn't until a few years later I realized I might be able to make money at it. Every year they had a home show at the Convention Hall downtown. There would be 30-foot display booths throughout the hall — one might be a new toilet bowl, another might be Venetian blinds — all kinds of products for the home. I'd go early in the morning and photograph the salesmen in their booths, using the pitch, "You don't have to pay now, there's no obligation," etc. Then I'd go home and make 8-by-10 prints, realizing it only cost 50 cents — and that I could sell them for $1. So I'd go back the next day and sell these prints to the salesmen. It became more than just business, though — I did begin to enjoy it. There is an aspect of alchemy in photography — a darkened room, working with liquids. It seemed very magical to me.

I went to Cooley High School. High school is an awkward time for most people; in my case I was overweight and was not comfortable relating to people. I was in trouble scholastically, getting low grades and skipping classes. At the time there weren't a lot of role models inspiring people to go to college — many of my friends back then didn't care if they finished high school. At some point, though, it was negotiated that I'd be the student helper and photograph the sporting events. This gave me a great sense of purpose. It really helped me socialize in a way I wouldn't have otherwise, because I'd take pictures at the basketball or football games, and afterwards, the athletes were always excited to see the photos. From there I ended up working part time at Royal Studios out on Seven Mile Road. They did portraits and wedding photos. I kept getting sucked into photography more and more. In my senior year at Cooley I got involved with some really nice students who actually talked about going to college. That was something that had

never occurred to me before. But that was when I decided I wanted to study photography. I began working endless hours at Federal Department Stores to save for college. And I did go — first to Rochester Institute of Technology, which was one of the few schools that had a program in photography. They really expanded my view of what photography could be — a means of individual creative expression. Since that time, I've been successful beyond my wildest dreams.

"

There is an aspect of alchemy in photography

— a darkened room, working with liquids. It seemed very magical to me.

"

Peter Karmanos Jr. is co-founder, chairman and CEO of Compuware Corporation.
Photographed at Compuware headquarters in Farmington Hills.

Back before cruising was a big thing on Woodward, a group of friends and I would go out cruising at night. We always had a hot car to get around in. Plymouth Furys. Chevy Impalas. At the time, I had a '58 Ford with dual four-barrel carburetors. We would cruise through a circuit of drive-ins, and sometimes finish it up with a ride down Woodward as well. We'd start at Richard's Drive-In, which was at Six Mile and Grand River. Then we'd take Grand River over to Lahser and go north to Eight Mile, and stop at the Richard's Drive-In at Eight Mile and Lahser. Then we'd head down Eight Mile Road to Greenfield; there was also a Richard's at Greenfield and Eight Mile. So we'd make that circuit, and every once in a while we'd run on over to Woodward and see if we could find a drag race. Then we'd tour all the drive-ins along Woodward, like The Maverick, and Ted's.

My parents had a restaurant around Grand River and Lahser. It was named Grand-Lahser Hamburger, but everybody called it Pete's. The 16th Precinct was also in that area, so all the police officers would come into the restaurant, and because I worked there, I got to know all of them.

One of those nights when my friends and I were out cruising, at about two in the morning, I got caught with some beer in the car. The police took me into the station and called my dad to come get me. I was up in the precinct area waiting for my dad to get there, and being 16 years old and having a lot of opinions about authority, I told the police what I thought about them. They finally said, "You're going back into the holding cell." So I went back and sat in the holding cell.

Eventually my dad walked in. I was the same size I am now — about 5 feet 11 inches — and my dad was 5 feet 6 inches. One of the officers brought me out of the holding cell, and my dad reached up and grabbed me by my shirt and gave me a slap. "I never want to have to come back here and get you again," he said. And all the police started cheering. "Don't even look at them," my dad whispered. "I'm going to turn around and I'm going to walk out of here, and you're going to walk right after me. I don't want you to say a word."

The police officers were all still cat-calling and cheering and calling me a jailhouse lawyer and all that stuff. We walked out and got into my dad's car, and he was very, very quiet. Dad started the car and was driving home; at that time we lived in northwest Detroit, around Seven Mile and Evergreen, so to get to our house there was a little bit of a ride. A few minutes went by, and it seemed like an eternity to me, it was so quiet. Finally he said, "You know, Peter, there are three kinds of people in this world. There are people who learn things the easy way, people who learn things the hard way, and then there are some poor people who never learn at all. All I'm trying to figure out is which of the last two groups you are." At the time, I thought that was pretty funny. But the more I thought about it, and the more I learned, the more I realized how right he was.

Ed Love is a radio personality.
Photographed at the WDET studios in Detroit.

I moved to Detroit on December 19, 1960. Back then, my favorite place to hear live jazz was a place called the Minor Key. It was over on Dexter near Burlingame. It was like a big coffeehouse, a huge coffeehouse, as far as attendance. They didn't serve alcohol, although I would suspect that there were times people brought in their own, but nobody went around checking. They assumed everyone came in there to listen to the music. That's what I went there for, I'll tell you that. It was a nice place, run by a guy named Sam, and some other people from what was left of the hippie movement. They had all kinds of exotic coffee, and people would pay high prices for it. You might have to pay a dollar or two for a cup of coffee, but you would go into the place and hear Miles Davis, John Coltrane, Stan Getz for $2, and stay in there all night if you wanted to. The bands would start playing at nine and on weekends wouldn't stop until five in the morning. Since they had no liquor license, they didn't have to close. And I mean these were big groups. During the days of the Minor Key, no club compared. Miles Davis had a home there. John Coltrane. You name them, and they had them. I saw the Duke Ellington Orchestra in there. The Maynard Ferguson Orchestra. And these people didn't just come for the weekend. They came in for a whole week. Some groups stayed there two weeks. Miles Davis must have rotated his appearances there every three or four months. The late Cannonball Adderley played there; he was a good friend of mine. I was sitting there one night listening to the music at about 3:30 in the morning. I was sleepy. And the music was loud, not irritating, but loud, just by the nature of the music. I fell asleep, so Cannonball Adderley came down and just hit me on the back of the head and said, "Hey, mother_____!" You can imagine the word he used. "How dare you sleep on my music. I'm going to sit here and make sure you don't sleep during the break." He was kidding, of course. I saw a lot happen in there. But that's what Detroit was to me.

I hear people talk about the Bluebird on Tireman and Beechwood on the west side in the '50s, which must have been wonderful. I know they had the hippest jukebox of any place in any city I have worked, because the box was all jazz. A lot of musicians like Roy Brooks, Barry Harris and Charles McPherson grew up in that area. Also Wendell Harrison, who is one of the giants of the Detroit jazz scene today. These young guys couldn't get in, but countless musicians tell the story about how Elvin Jones, the great drummer — who was the house drummer at that time at the Bluebird — would help them out. Drums are almost always situated at the back of the band, so Elvin was sitting at the back, which was by the window. These young guys knew that. On hot summer nights the young aspiring jazz drummers would go up to that window at the back of the building. Elvin always knew they were there, and he would pull the curtain back so they could see what was going on, so the drummers would watch Elvin and see what he was doing with his hands and feet. Now and then on Sundays they had family days at the Bluebird, and they'd let the young kids come in and Elvin would be there letting them play his drums. And the other young guys would play other instruments. Many of them told me that was the greatest experience they had ever had, getting up there when they were just teenagers playing alongside some of the giants and future giants of jazz.

I would imagine that the Minor Key in the '60s would have taken the place of what the Bluebird was in the '50s. They did a great job at the Minor Key. It didn't last long enough, though. I often wish the Minor Key were still open so other people could see it. I talk about it on the air, but you had to be there to really know what it was. It was really something.

Shirley Muldowney is a top fuel dragster driver.

Photographed at the Raceway Park in Old Bridge Township, New Jersey.

It was the Motor City. Every "dreamer" standing at the guardrail wanted to be a driver. Detroit Dragway was all we heard about back east. I had arrived here in 1971, and from the first time I set eyes on "Big Daddy" Don Garlits, the man who started it all, I wanted to drive a nitro-burning fuel dragster more than anything else in the world. Racecars really didn't get a lot of attention if you were based on the East Coast, as I started my career on the streets of Schenectady, New York. You had to be centrally located, and certainly the Motor City, as far as I was concerned, was the watering hole of it all. So I moved to Detroit and never looked back — it was one of the things I did right in the early days.

The Detroit Dragway was really kind of a dump. But it had its history. It had its following. The food was barely edible and the restrooms were far from decent. For the racers, it was dangerous. But one thing for sure, they packed them in. On a Saturday night, there was barely standing room only. It was all the fans had to get their "nitro fix," and the people really supported it. In just a short period of time, the promoter became a very rich man. Today we have these mega-speedways, beautiful facilities that cater to the fans and racers. But back then all we had was a mud hole at Sibley and Dix. We raced on a marginal surface without safe guardrail or sufficient shutdown. It was primitive, but the racers always gave the fans what they paid for in the early days, and fans were willing to get down and dirty to see these cars run 200 mph in a quarter mile, just as we were to drive them. Little did we know how we were really sticking our necks out. Always frustrating was the long wait at the pay window, but that, too, went with the times. Those were the '70s. Thank God we survived to race in the '90s.

The fans at Detroit Dragway all wanted to be sitting where we drivers were sitting. That was one of the differences in the Detroit fans in the early days. They were so close to it — yet so far away. As drivers, we would think, *stand back, get out of my way, let me show you how it's done.* But looking back now, the fans had every right in the world to want to be where we were. At 59 years old today, still able to do what I do best, I can now appreciate it when a fan comes up to me and says, "Man, I gotta do this somehow, some way — I'm gonna be just like you. I'm going to be the next Shirley." And they're dead serious.

I think part of the reason for the passion of those fans was in the ads they ran on the radio. They were much different than the radio ads you would hear any place else in the country. They would start out with, "Sunday! Sunday! Sunday! Come see Kalitta, Garlits, Muldowney ..." and they'd name all the racers entered. But through the ad, you would hear a fuel dragster engine running at an idle in the background. And if you've never heard a fuel "motor" you haven't lived. It's a sound that's unmistakable. You know exactly what it is. I still have fans in their 50s and 60s mention those ads all the time. There's no doubt it helped bring spectators in the gate.

Today it's much different. To see the cars on television doesn't capture the sound or the feel of when two cars leave the starting line. With their combined 12,000 horsepower, they truly shake the ground beneath your feet. Back then the engines produced 4,000 horsepower.

That was the legacy Detroit Dragway left for fans. For drivers, there was another legacy. Racers, then and now, know what hard work is. In order to survive, you must pay attention on and off the track. "You can't play when you've gotta pay" is the way we used to address it. That means work on your equipment, get it ready, correct it, find out what the problems are in terms of your combination. Then fix it and get it ready for another track with a whole different set of conditions like altitude, atmosphere, track temperature, etc. All these things are important to a winning combination, and every track is different. So it's constant work and maintenance. Racing on the older speedways, like Detroit Dragway, certainly came with its unique combination. Everybody has to pay their dues in one way or another. You had to go out there and learn on your own. The one thing that I still have going for me is the experience I had on the older tracks. I definitely learned the hard way and it gave me the respect you need when driving the 300-mph cars of today. When you look back at tracks such as Detroit Dragway, you have to realize that the sport of drag racing has come a long, long way. Today's super speedways are basically all the same, so the younger drivers don't have the experience they need when faced with a marginal racetrack. Knowing how to deal with less-than-perfect conditions definitely separates the men from the boys.

I'm getting ready to run Motor City's Milan Dragway on my birthday, June 19. It's a Saturday-night show, and they will pack them in the stands. Milan always does. I'll run against one of the best competitors out there, driving Don Prudhomme's car. He's a nice young man and a fine driver, one of the best. But now he's faced with running a smaller track, something he doesn't do very often, and I'm sure he's worried. Not worried that he's going to get hurt, but that he's going to lose. It's a good racetrack, far better than Detroit Dragway. But by today's standards, in comparison, it's not considered a super speedway. This young driver asked IHRA World Champion Paul Romine what he thought his chances were racing Shirley there, and Paul said, "Well, I'll tell ya. It's a little short, it's a little narrow, it's a little dark, and Shirley is gonna whip your ass." The guy's eyes got real big as Paul continued to pull his leg a little bit. The kid and his team are certainly capable of winning the race, but smart enough to know that they definitely have their work cut out for them, considering we've set Milan's track record for speed three years in a row.

Looking back today, it's disappointing that we didn't have a better arena than Detroit Dragway to showcase our talent, but it's sure been fun to watch the sport grow into one of, if not *the* most exciting form of motorsports there is. When you consider what we all came from, just a bunch of kids racing on the streets, one has to be impressed. Back then, I never thought that someday the doors would be wide open for lady drivers. Little did I realize what this was all going to turn into on Sunday! Sunday! Sunday!

"

The food was barely edible and the restrooms

were far from decent. For the racers, it was dangerous.

But one thing for sure, they packed them in.

"

John Lee Hooker is a blues musician.
Photographed at his home in the suburbs of San Francisco, California.

I'm from Detroit. I wasn't born there, but I grew up there, you know. When I arrived I was a young thing, not 21 yet. I used to play around the city — that was a long time ago.

I left the South and I headed north. I could have tried Chicago, but there was too much activity there, with the blues singing — I kept going north. In Detroit, I would have been known as the only blues singer around, but Chicago was loaded with them — just on and on in Chicago. So I figured if I wanted a chance I'd come to Detroit. And that's where I got turned on to it.

I had a job on the side at a steel mill — Copco Steel — during the day. Then, every weekend for three years I'd be jamming at the Apex Bar, when I first started out. That was on Russell Street on the north end of Detroit. I wasn't even old enough to get in there. "Boom Boom," you heard that number? I wrote it when I was working there. A girl named Willow, she was the bartender at the Apex Bar, and I'd be late comin' in. The band would be already there, waiting for me. I'd come in with my guitar, she'd say, "You're late again. Boom, boom boom. You're late again." I made a song out of it. "Boom boom boom boom. Shoot you right down. How how how how. Boom." I made my living there until I got famous.

Elmer Barbee discovered me — he had a record store, he heard me, and he wanted to record me. We'd just do whatever we could. Once or twice a week, we drank wine, recorded a little, all the stuff that you heard, like "Boogie Chillen," I did down at his place.

"Boom Boom," "Boogie Chillen," "I Cover the Waterfront" — the deep blues all came out of my time in Detroit. It was an automatic gift. I didn't write it down in a book anywhere. It's in my head and heart. In my heart and soul. They come to me and it's a gift, to be able to remember them. Any song you hear me do, I didn't get out of no book.

I love Detroit, still do, I love it, I firmly do. Don't like the cold weather there anymore, though.

When I first arrived I thought it was a big, big city. I was a country boy, thought I'd find the blues, and get famous. That's what I thought. I found Detroit was the place I wanted to stay. My career grew, I grew up, lived there, got married, had kids, then got divorced in that town and became a free, single man, with no one to talk to. This town has really been good to me.

Sonny Eliot is a meteorologist, author and pilot.
Photographed at his office above Lindell AC in Detroit.

Television happened on the scene in Detroit in 1947. That July, I did my very first television show, called *Open House*. There were something like 2,500 television sets in the entire state of Michigan at the time.

There used to be a nightclub called Club 509 on the corner of Woodward, near Jefferson. The staff consisted of an emcee named Dick Havilland and his chorus line (I always said they were a chorus line of eight, and some were a little older). Anyway, that staff was on the show, *Open House*. Part of it was a routine between George Scotty, a pantomimist who lip-synched records, and me. We were doing all kinds of variety shows, children's shows, talk shows, sports shows, all these things, and they suddenly discovered that people were interested in weather.

They set aside a couple minutes for weather in the newscast, and I thought, gee, that's my background. As a pilot in the Air Force, I had all this training in weather. So I asked them if I could take a whack at it, and they said, "Let's do it." Of course I breezed through it because it was something I'd been doing. I did it on a very technical basis — 500 millibar charts, prog charts, relative and absolute humidity, isobars, isotherms, all the things that technical people do. For about three months I labored through the technical jargon of meteorology. Things like what the adiobatic lapse rate was, why three-and-a-half degrees per thousand feet and not five degrees per thousand feet, what causes rain, what freezing rain is and how it's formed and so on. Then one day I gave a temperature in Las Vegas. "It's 55 degrees in Las Vegas. 5 and 5. That's ten the hard way." And it got a chuckle. I gave a temperature from Florida, "where

businessmen lie on the beach all day long. They lie about their age, lie about all kinds of things." I found lines like that relieved the pressure and made the reports more palatable. Through the years I developed several gimmicks. Like portmanteau words. Cloudy and cool. *Clool*. Rain and Drizzle. *Raizzle*. Snow and fog. *Snog*.

I used jokes, too, such as, "A hunter followed some tracks into a cave. And shot a train." Viewers would respond to that. People might ask, "How could they respond to something that corny?" And the truth of the matter is, people love corn. They're just ashamed to admit it. I like corny stuff myself. If you want to feel superior, you say, "that's corny." And secretly you enjoy it. It's a guilty pleasure. I found that if I prefaced whatever I was doing with a smart-aleck line I had discovered, or one that I made up, or one that I enjoyed, the show developed what I considered a little personality. When I was a student at Wayne State, if I had a professor that was entertaining as well as dispensing information, I really absorbed a great deal more. So I tried to apply that to a weather show. My reports became more of a show, and I would work on them as I would work on any entertainment piece. Television is primarily an entertainment medium. It is secondarily an information medium. If you combine the two, you've got the right combination. To get the right balance is what's difficult.

Once I made a prediction that we'd have a fairly decent day with a few snow flurries. And we had something like eleven inches of snow. Paul Williams, Don Kremer and some of the other people who were on the newscast went through the building and got all kinds of rubber galoshes and overshoes and things like that. And they filled the snow bag full of them. (A snow bag is a big canvas thing they keep overhead on the set, fill it and shake it out — and snow or whatever is in it comes down.) The next night, I came on and my opening line was something like, "Well, we all make mistakes, and that's why the welcome mat never gets dusty at Jackson Prison. I predicted snow flurries yesterday and today we had eleven inches of snow, I'm sorry!" When I said that, they opened the snow bag and hundreds of galoshes and overshoes and gloves fell on me and buried me.

The weatherman was the welcome relief from the hard news of the day. They could take shots at the weatherman, who was never right. He was actually almost *always* right, when you look back in the record. 80 percent of the time the weather was predicted correctly. Even more so now, with satellite and the technology they have today. Over the years, it's been a marvelous ride in the city of Detroit. In the mornings, I used to get up, look out the great big window I had in my apartment and say, "I'll lick you yet, Detroit." For laughs, of course. Detroit has been very good to me.

u

Once I made a prediction that we'd have

a fairly decent day with a few snow flurries.

And we had something like eleven inches of snow.

n

Judge Cornelia Kennedy serves on the United States Court of Appeals.
Photographed in the chief judge's courtroom in Detroit.

I grew up on Grandmont Street in the Rosedale area. I'd always considered being a lawyer. My father was a lawyer, and my mother was going to law school when she died. It was very different than it is today. There were not a lot of women in law school, but it wasn't because they weren't admitted; it was because they just didn't apply. In my experience, I thought the professors were, for the most part, very fair. They called on me in class, and I got good grades. I didn't really think about being a woman; I just went to law school. Some things were hard — I couldn't walk in the front door of the Michigan Union across the street. And I couldn't live in the Law Quad — only men could live there. So I had to live a mile away at Stockwell Hall, a place for graduate women. That meant that I had to walk that mile three times a day back and forth. I figure that's why I'm healthy — I really did a lot of walking. It was pretty cold at times, too.

When I first began to practice law, sometimes I was the only woman in the courtroom, unless it was a jury trial and there were women on the jury. It was a little hard in those days to make people realize that I was a lawyer. I remember in the early '50s attending a convention of a lawyers' organization in Boston with my senior partner, and people thought I was his secretary. Even after I got on the circuit court, we would go to judges' meetings, somebody would introduce me saying, "This is Judge Kennedy," and the person I was being introduced to would try to shake hands with my husband. There weren't very many women judges when I started out. Of course, that's not the case any longer. But early '70s even, it was rare.

We had our methods of networking, though. For several years, back in the '50s, we assembled a group of 15 or 20 women lawyers and put on a little show every year for the judges in the circuit court and Recorder's Court. Henrietta Rosenthal, who was one of the early women lawyers in Detroit, and the first women to be prosecutor, would take Gilbert and Sullivan songs and write new lyrics for them. She was really clever; she'd write different parodies for us to sing. Then we would practice over at the GAR Building on Grand River — Grand Army of the Republic, for the Civil War veterans. It's closed now, although the building itself is still there. We'd either practice there or the county jail, because they had a piano in the chapel. I think that was the first time I ever went to the county jail. Those were the only two places we could find to rehearse. None of us could sing or dance, so it was done all in fun. Each year we'd perform in a hotel, like the Statler or the Book Cadillac; we'd have a dinner and then give the performance. That was how we gave women lawyers an opportunity to meet judges. That was the idea.

It's really nice now to have more women in the courts. While it was rare being a woman lawyer when I started practicing, the men, the other judges, were helpful. I can't say that there was anybody that didn't treat me fairly; I never had any real problems. You can't be just like other people, because you're not like other people. We're all different. Of course, all the men are different, too. I really loved it; I loved all my years of judging, and I loved practicing law. Of course, there were difficult lawyers, difficult litigants and really hard problems you don't know how to solve, but I've really been fortunate, because I've liked everything that I've ever done. I could have taken senior status 10 years ago, and I would have had a substantial increase in my net worth, so you can tell I like it. I guess I wouldn't know what to do if I retired. Sometimes I look out the window here and it's hard to believe that I've come downtown to work almost every day for nearly 50 years.

Dr. Jai Krishna Prasad is a burn surgeon.
Photographed at Detroit Receiving Hospital in Detroit.

I came to Detroit in 1976 — and now I know my way around. But before that, when I was living in London, Ontario, it was a different story. One November evening, I drove down with my wife and three children to visit a friend at the Detroit Medical Center (DMC), a urologist named Dr. Sinha. He's now in private practice; in those days he was doing work with the head of urology at DMC, doing kidney transplants.

Dr. Sinha had given me directions, but when I came out of the Tunnel and was looking for the Lodge Freeway, I somehow got lost. I came to Jefferson, and instead of making the U-turn on Jefferson where you can get the Lodge Freeway, I went a little farther, a quarter of a mile, and somehow or another, I can't figure it out, I ended up on Gratiot. And after that it was one mistake after another; the more I drove I just kept getting deeper into the mistake. I had no idea where I was going or what was happening to me. So I stopped at different gas stations and different places, and everybody I asked tried to help me. But I got so many different directions from so many different people, I got more and more confused. It was quite an experience.

Finally, my son said from the back seat, "Dad, why do you have your window down? Isn't Detroit a dangerous city?" (That was his perception, from not having lived here.) "Don't worry," I answered him. "The Lord will take care of us and lead us where we need to go."

It must have been very apparent how lost we were, because a short time later, a green Volkswagen pulled up to us — it was a black couple who had given us directions a while back. They had watched and seen that I couldn't follow their directions, so they said, "Follow us, we'll lead you to the Lodge Freeway." Under certain circumstances, if you get compassionate help you can never forget it. This couple was very, very kind and gracious and so understanding that even though it has been 23 years, their act is still very vivid in my memory.

They led me to the Lodge Freeway, and I finally found my way to my friend, Dr. Sinha. That experience proved to me that generalization of people is wrong.

When I first came to the area, I worked in Ann Arbor. Later, when I moved to DMC in Detroit, they told me that my patients would be nothing like the ones I had in Ann Arbor. And they were right. Being here in the city of Detroit and dealing with burn patients has been a very rewarding experience, because many patients don't have any financial resources or family resources. So you have to find different ways to treat them, getting funding from firefighters and other organizations, to be able to afford to give them supplies and try to make sure they follow up despite the fact that they don't have any support system. We see frostbite patients from homeless shelters. Because shelters won't keep people in the daytime, there are homeless who go out on the street in sub-zero temperatures at six in the morning and walk in the street with wet socks and holes in their shoes. By the time they come back in the evening they have frostbite. And they'll do the same thing the next day. So the cycle of freeze and thaw, freeze and thaw, freeze and thaw causes gangrene of the toes and fingers, and many, many patients have to have amputations. In the winter of 1993 we saw 30 to 40 frostbite patients. I started a program where I go to the shelters and give a presentation on how to prevent frostbite. The Detroit Red Wings helped us by collecting mittens, gloves and shoes at their home games, so that when we started work at the shelters we took bags of them so the homeless could protect themselves. As a result, the number of frostbite cases has decreased. These opportunities have been a great privilege to me, because I am able to take part in helping people. A doctor's glory is not in studies or awards — it is entirely in your patients. So the opportunities the people of Detroit have given me to make a difference in their lives is a very important part of my life.

Serving the people of Detroit has also been rewarding to me from the standpoint of learning more about the nature of people and this country. I am from India originally, which is a very rich culture. But the United States is a melting pot, where a new civilization is being built. America is where we are breaking down the boundaries. We need to look at human beings as a whole, not just their appearance. Dr. Martin Luther King said content of character is what makes life worth living. I came here to learn about America — and there are truly different worlds, the suburbs and the city. Had I stayed in Ann Arbor, I would have known less than half of what this country and this city are about.

"

When I moved to DMC in Detroit,

they told me that my patients would be nothing

like the ones I had in Ann Arbor.

And they were right.

"

Thom Sharp is an alleged actor/comedian.

Photographed on the set of Home Improvement, Disney Studio, in Los Angeles, California.

It was a hot summer night long, long ago in a galaxy far, far away. Yes, the night in 1965 when Skip Beuckelaere (even he can't pronounce his name) and I were rousted out of Grosse Pointe and told never to return.

Skip, who is now a designer at Ford, owned the ugliest car in Detroit in 1965: a pink, rusted, beat-up 1959 Rambler with no shocks. At some point, before Skip bought the car, it had been painted with a brush. Anyway, we were a couple of West Side kids who figured it was a good time to explore the other side of town. The East Side. Grosse Pointe. The land of penny loafers and trust funds.

We set off down the Edsel Ford Expressway, past the Kelsey Hayes plant ... it always smelled like a bad mixture of E&B Beer, kielbasa and a squirrely digestive system. Quick, roll up the windows. Okay, we're past. Quick, roll *down* the windows. It's a humid 96 degrees and moss is growing on the north side of my face.

From the Edsel Ford, we hung a big right on the Lodge Freeway (why is the Ford an expressway and the Lodge a freeway?). Past the Wonder Bread Bakery. Quick, leave the windows down. Boy, that spot on the freeway smelled good, didn't it?

By now, Big Pink had carried us all the way to downtown Detroit. Ah, downtown in the '60s. Before the People Mover. Before The Fist. Before Hudson's was blown up. Before Woodward turned into one long string of wig shops. Actually, I could use a wig.

We were flying now. Skip's pink Rambler could hit 48 mph with a following wind, and we were getting a nice one off the river. On Jefferson, we cruised past all of the streets that my mother used to talk about ... Chene, Mt. Elliott, Crane. She grew up on Crane around the time of World War I (now the street looks like it had been *in* World War I. And II).

Almost to Grosse Pointe now (I think the "e" on the end of "Pointe" is for "elite" or "exclusive," or maybe just "eat it"). The first sign said "Grosse Pointe Park." This is where the assistant snobs lived. Couldn't quite afford the better Pointes.

The sign for "Grosse Pointe" proper was just ahead. The houses were getting better. Much better. We're talking estates. Skip and I were like the Clampetts, driving into Beverly Hills looking for debutantes. There was a Ford woman right over that hedge. We just knew it.

We were speeding along at about 31 mph when we saw the flashing lights of the squad car behind us. Along with the blinding light of that tractor beam they're so fond of. And the bullhorn was a nice touch: "Pull over you scum-sucking pricks from Downriver in the car that couldn't possibly be from one of the Pointes and therefore you must be here to break into somebody's house like a Stroh or a Dodge." I'm paraphrasing, but you get the idea.

Skip and I were rousted out of Big Pink. But, officer. Our hands slapped to the roof of the car. A hunk of rust dropped into the back seat. Officer, you don't understand. Legs spread apart. Frisked. Portable tractor beam blasted into our eyes. Possible retina damage. Did we know where we *were?* THIS IS GROSSE POINTE, YOU PUNKS! GET THE F&%# OUT OF HERE AND DON'T EVER COME BACK!

And I haven't. Well, once. My car was parked on Kercheval; a guy broke in and put in a nicer radio. And on my way back across the Grosse Pointe border, I got a ticket for driving a car without an Interior Trim Package. Some things never change.

Tyree Guyton is an artist.
Photographed at the Heidelberg Project in Detroit.

TYREE GUYTON

At the age of nine, a young boy was given a paintbrush and declared it was like his hand was on fire. That was me. I knew immediately I wanted to be an artist. Today, 34 years later, I have become known for the controversial artscape known as the Heidelberg Project.

I began the project in 1986, and this block on Detroit's east side has become an explosion in cast-offs and color. I saw a need in my community to speak out against social and economic injustices.

Armed with a paintbrush and a broom, I began by cleaning up abandoned houses and vacant lots on Heidelberg Street. From the rubble I accumulated, I affixed found and discarded objects to the houses. Gradually, abandoned houses became giant mixed-media sculptures, and vacant lots literally became "lots of art." I called it the Heidelberg Project and, yes, I dared to call it art!

Neighbors came alive in a way I hadn't witnessed since I was a boy. Some of them liked it and called it art. Some of them loathed it and called me crazy. Whether pro or con, one thing was certain, people were coming from all over the world to witness this much-talked-about and highly publicized art/junk creation.

I wanted to use my talent to bring about positive change in my community. And you can't bring about real change without controversy. Detroit is striving for a comeback, a world-class city, if you will. To me, casinos and ball stadiums, tearing down old, significant buildings for copycat developments that look like they belong anywhere but here, is like putting old wine in new skins. My vision is to create an artistic haven. I organized the Heidelberg Project as a non-profit community arts project, but many funders and city leaders have been perplexed by it and split in their support of it. I have been praised for it, then torn down, praised again and torn down again. But I have withstood the test of time. I could have taken my vision anywhere to make it happen, but I believe it was supposed to happen here, in Detroit, the city of originality. It's time to take The Heidelberg Project to the next level. I believe this project can create jobs and bring a sense of pride back to the community. I have a vision for the common people, and it's working.

Dave Coulier is a comedian and actor.
Photographed at Notre Dame High School in Harper Woods, Michigan.

Well, my career in comedy really started on my parents' front porch in St. Clair Shores. I used to sit on the front porch with my brother, Dan, and we would watch the neighbors and do their voices and kind of make up conversations about what they were saying to each other. I remember we'd get each other laughing really hard.

And then we would lay in our bunk beds at night and we'd start doing these characters and reprise our favorite stories. That's kind of how it all started. Then I realized I could really make people laugh. I played sports my whole life, mostly hockey, and I was always the funny guy in the locker room. It's kind of like having a built-in audience. I'd do impressions of other players, or coaches, and when I would do that, the guys would laugh, and I started figuring out I can really do this.

Teachers just didn't know what to do with me. Here is this kid coming along, doing impressions of teachers, doing sound effects, telling weird stories. I didn't fit the curriculum of what kids were supposed to do. I was always kind of cracking kids up, making people laugh. It's just the way I've always been. I spent some time in the principal's office. And then the principal actually started to like me, so I'd get sent down and he'd say, "All right, what happened today?" When I'd tell him what happened, he'd say, "That's really kind of funny. Grab a magazine and go back to your next class."

It started next door in the cafeteria doing shows. Guys were skipping class to come and listen to my funny stories and impressions and things — it was in sixth period. I basically would tell these stories with all these made-up characters in them. I had this whole family called the Sauce Family that I had made up. Every day the story would start the same, and I would just kind of improvise some crazy story. One kid laughed so hard he threw up. And then we got an idea, me and eight

other guys that I thought were really funny that I used to hang out with here in school. We decided to put on a concert next door at the all-girl's Catholic high school, Regina, which is one driveway over. So we put together a whole production and did a comedy show and had about 800 people show up, which was really tremendous. It just kept propelling me that I was doing the right thing.

It was pretty amazing, because people were laughing. I realized, *Oh my gosh, this is really my dream, here I'm doing it in high school.* I used to do the announcements here in the morning. The principal, Mr. Vachon, he's quite a character. I used to do an impression of him in the mornings before school — "I'd like to know who the little shit is that set a goddamn bowl of chili in the bathroom." He sure got your attention. The teachers kind of got a kick out of it. They all wanted me to do an impression of them.

He also used to teach a creative writing class. That's where he and I became friends. He flunked me my four first papers. My fifth one, he came out and just ripped on me, and I thought, *Here I go, I'm going to get another F,* because all my papers were funny, and he'd give us really serious papers, like, "Do you know anyone who died in Vietnam and what was that like? Tell me about it, what do you know about death?" So I would write something funny about death, or something funny about Vietnam. I just kept writing funny stuff. By the fifth paper, he said, "I want you to read this." And he threw the paper at me. I thought I'd gotten an F. I actually got an A+ on this paper, and he wiped out all the other Fs. He said, "You have a style. The first papers, I thought you were a cynical little SOB. Then I started to realize that was your style, and you didn't stray from it even though you were getting Fs. That's a good thing."

DAVE COULIER

This paper was about an altar boy canoe trip. In eighth grade, this guy and I were just little stoners. We got ripped. We were having the best time; we raced ahead of anybody in the group. We went 35 miles that way, and the rest of the group went 35 miles in the opposite direction, so we were just hanging back, saying, "I wonder where everybody is." So it got to be nighttime, and they had to send the National Guard out in helicopters to find us. In the paper, I admitted we were ripped. It was just the truth. I wrote a funny story about it. A lot of kids didn't want to admit that they did anything like that, they thought they'd get in trouble. But I didn't care.

Another friend of mine, Mark Cendrowski, had been doing stuff since third grade, drawing pictures and doing comedy bits. We put together this show next door at the all-girls school. Now Mark's a sitcom director. He directs all kinds of sitcoms; he's a very sought-after TV director.

We said when we were little kids we were going to do comedy. And we both did it.

The first time I did a professional thing anywhere in the area, on a real stage, a real show, with drunk people, I opened for a local guy named Jim Freeman. He was kind of like a local comedian. It was terrible. About 10 minutes into my act, a waitress came up to me with a napkin with a request. It just said, "Get off." So I got off. But I remember Jim Freeman paid me $100, which was amazing. I never forgot that, it was really cool.

My favorite was a night in Windsor, Canada, I got three standing ovations. I didn't know what else to do after that. I think it was called the Comedy Corner. A tiny place.

When I came back here a few years ago, in 1988, the hockey program had gone under, it was no longer. And when I played here, this was a hockey dynasty. This school was a big ice hockey school. My defense partner played in the NHL. It was a really high-caliber hockey program, and being defunct, they decided to have me come and play a concert in the gym. It was called "Yuks for Pucks." Bob Probert and I signed autographs, I did a concert. It was a miserable summer day, it was probably about 110 degrees in the gym, they had the fans going — it was a really good thing. We donated all the money and brought back the hockey program. It was the school's idea. They said, "We're wondering if you would come and do a benefit." And I said, of course. And the school really needs a lot of help. The numbers have declined. They put it together, all I did was show up, step on stage and do a show. That's the way it happened.

I did do some crazy things here. My freshman year my locker partner streaked through the all-girls school next door with a ski mask on. That was quite a day. I was always the guy who got other kids to do funny things for my enjoyment. It was always funny stuff, though, nothing that would hurt anybody. Pulling your pants off and putting them on your head, you know, "I bet you won't walk through the whole school with your pants on your head." So that was the kind of kid I was.

I had some momentum, knew I wanted to do it. My family is really funny, they all love to laugh. My brother is actually one of the funniest people I know. There were lots of influences along the way. A lot of people said you're crazy, you're not going to get to Hollywood from St. Clair Shores, Michigan.

"

My freshman year my locker partner

streaked through the all-girls school

next door with a ski mask on.

That was quite a day.

"

Dr. Mat Dawson, Jr. is a skilled tradesman and philanthropist.
Photographed at Ford's River Rouge Plant.

My greatest memory is when I was hired here at Ford. It was September 30, 1940, and it was the greatest day of my life. I was 19, and I moved up here from Shreveport, Louisiana. I had two uncles working here at Ford, and listening to them talking, I decided I really wanted a job here. They told me it was a good place to work, told me they paid well, so I wanted to be a part of the organization myself. I got on a bus and came up to Detroit. The trip took about two days; my uncles met me at the station.

I was hired in the pressed steel building (which is the Stamping Plant now) by the late Mr. Don Marshall, an African-American man. He was head of the personnel department and labor relations. He took care of the blacks; Mr. Miller took care of the whites. Mr. Marshall and Mr. Miller didn't work a desk — they didn't sit down. They were enclosed in a steel cage with wire all around it. They stood all day long behind a tall desk — they were timekeepers. If you got in trouble, you had to go and see them. That was the setup back in those days.

I started work the next day at 7 a.m. In some ways, it was just another job, but it was exciting to me. They trained me as a press operator, stamping out doors. It wasn't hard to learn, but you had to watch yourself and each other, so you didn't get hurt. They were big presses.

Then the UAW struck. It was 1941. And they meant business. I had been laid off from the pressed steel building, then they transferred me to the iron foundry. That was exciting work — I worked on the crankshaft job, the midnight shift. And that's where I was working when they shut the place down at three o'clock in the morning. The UAW had people coming here from all over the United States to help organize this place. A lot of people lost their lives. People demonstrated, and they were turning over cars and everything. Anybody who wanted to come in here had to fight to do it. I think we were on strike about two weeks before they finally agreed to the union to have a national labor relation election in here. And they held the election right here inside the plant with state troopers guarding the ballot box.

The plant was closed for close to a month because we had to go through elections and voting and negotiate a contract. I was glad to go back; we had won a contract. Union dues were a dollar a month. Now it's two hours of your wages every month. To me, it's worth it. It was one of the greatest things that could have happened. People back then were all divided. Especially African-Americans. Some of them didn't think they would get justice out of the union, some of them figured that the company was good enough to them as it was. But the end result was good because it put everybody on an equal base. Back then, if they needed to lay somebody off, they would lay off whoever they wanted. And they would pay you what they wanted to pay you. If I'm working beside you, doing the same job you're doing, I'm supposed to make the same money you're doing. It didn't always work that way before the union came in, though. Now people's jobs are all classified, and that's what we get paid for. And to me, just having seniority rights alone is worth the monthly dues!

I'm just proud to be a part of the Ford Motor Company. I'm proud of the Ford product. I drive a '95 Ford Escort. I have always invested in Ford, all they give me. I saved and invested. I used to own big cars, Continentals, big homes and things, but that doesn't excite me now. I'd rather leave a legacy. I've had many jobs here at Ford; I've worked all over. And I've been a rigger for thirty years. I learned to do my job and mind my own business. I'm not too much of a group man. I'm more of an individual person. But I enjoy my work, I enjoy my friends, and I just look forward to coming here every day. It keeps me active, keeps me living.

Jimmie Thompson is an artist.
Photographed at The Parade Company in Detroit.

JIMMIE THOMPSON

I'm a third-generation Detroit artist — my grandfather, my father and now me.

My father owned Academy Studios, a commercial art studio down on West Grand Boulevard. His true love was painting, so at home he would do his oil paintings and fill every birthday card with great cartoons and drawings. I would always look forward to the cards. But for a living, he developed this great company; it was in a real cool area in a great time period. Back in the early '60s, when I was about four or five years old, on Saturdays and Sundays he would take me down there. He needed to finish up work, and I think he took me along because he wanted to get me out of my mom's hair. As he finished up whatever he was doing while the other employees weren't there, I would end up sitting at one of the drawing tables, getting used to all the different art supplies. So I felt like I had my own little art studio.

The building was right next to the GM building and across from the Fisher Theatre; it was a great environment. Dad's studio was on the top floor of the Lexington Hotel. Staying down below in the hotel would be a lot of the stars that were playing at the Fisher Theatre, and I would hear my father talk about meeting them in the elevator. I got to know a lot of the people in the building; there was a restaurant down below where a woman would make cakes for our birthdays, so that whole little area near Woodward seemed very familiar to me, very welcoming. Motown was right down the street, too. We would hear the hits they produced on the radio; although at the time, I didn't really understand how significant that was.

The outside of the building is vague to me now, because when I was outside, there were so many surrounding buildings, and from my perspective as a little boy I just saw this whole ocean of buildings. I do remember the Lexington Hotel was a fairly prestigious hotel at the time, and the front of it had kind of the look of an east or west Central Park entrance. The back of it was much less appealing; it had the whole urban alley look. You had this great front, a façade, and in the back was a Dumpster and valet parking, where a gentleman looked after people's cars from a small booth. So it was kind of two worlds, same building. That building is no longer there — now it's a park. I've gone down for TasteFest and have seen bands playing there, and I thought, *That's kind of cool; that's on the same spot that my dad's business was.*

I remember the inside better. The floor layout was broken up, because it was originally a hotel — and still was down below. So a lot of the rooms were split up from its hotel days. They had done some renovation, though, and opened up certain parts to form a board meeting room and areas for layout artists and keyliners. My favorite place was the darkroom, where they did all their photography. After they had done a photo shoot, I loved watching the whole process of developing the photos, cropping them down and cleaning up different areas and changing them so they would be all set up for the press.

Mostly I loved drawing, so for me it was perfect because I had access to all the markers and paints and paper I could imagine. Plus, I had this view of the city from the top of this building just a block or two away from Woodward, giving me this whole landscape that I could draw. My father never pushed me to be an artist, but he always encouraged it, so it was really kind of an exciting thing to go down there on a Saturday and Sunday. I always liked drawing characters; I loved to illustrate books. And my dad was very supportive. As opposed to forcing different techniques, he would say, "I might do it this way," or "Someone might do it this way," and show me different styles other people had done. That's how he showed me that there was more than one way to illustrate, without being pushy about it. He was very soft spoken, but clever and intuitive in his own way — he was probably one of my biggest influences because of his demeanor, his talent and the way he would relate to people. His employees liked him, and he would tend to draw people in to the things that he was saying.

After he had gotten his work done and I'd done about a ream's worth of drawings, we'd either go to Lewis Artist Supply, the DIA or Sanders or some other place on or around Woodward. First of all, having the bird's-eye view of the area, then drawing it, and finally going down and hanging out was really wonderful.

My father and mother were married in a church on Woodward, my wife and I were married in the City-County Building on Woodward, my house in Ferndale is a block away from Woodward, and the job I held for over a decade revolved around designing parades to go down that street. I guess you could say my life is sort of a Woodward in Wonderland.

"

Staying down below in the hotel would be a lot of the stars

that were playing at the Fisher Theater, and I would hear my

father talk about meeting them in the elevator.

"

Jerod Swallow and Elizabeth Punsalan are five-time U.S. national ice dancing champions.
Photographed at Wing Lake, Bloomfield Township.

JEROD SWALLOW & ELIZABETH PUNSALAN

We spend a lot of time traveling now, usually touring with *Champions On Ice*, which comes to Joe Louis Arena every spring. Each year our families and friends come downtown to watch us perform. It's a great chance for them to see us skate live, and in a much more relaxed atmosphere than when we were skating competitively. We can definitely tell we're skating for a hometown crowd at The Joe. The older arenas are the favorites for performers because the seats are situated on a steeper grade, which makes the noise reverberate throughout the building. And we feed off of that noise during our performance, usually putting in extra energy from all of the adrenalin. Joe Louis is good and loud, and the Detroit fans are the best.

Some skaters never get to compete in their hometown. But in January of 1994, Detroit hosted the National Figure Skating Championships, which were also our Olympic trials. Mayor Archer had just been elected, so it was an exciting time for the city. And for us, it was another chance to make the Olympic team after having been alternates with a disappointing third place finish in 1992. Everyone we had ever known was at this event. Friends and family were driving the vans to the rink, working in registration, monitoring practice sessions, etc. This particular competition was very nerve-wracking, due to the fact that there was only one spot for the Olympic team, and that everyone we had ever known was at this event. We ended up skating one of the very few "performances of a lifetime," and earned our berth on the Olympic team in front of everyone we had ever known. And that felt amazing.

We could really hear the hometown crowd that night.

Having figure-skating events at the Joe Louis Arena has also created a great parallel of support between figure skating and hockey. We are huge Red Wings fans. We've caught a lot of games on the road; our paths cross quite a bit. And there are Red Wings jerseys at every game — no matter what city we're in, everybody is rooting for them. Some of the Russian skaters we travel with have grown up with these guys, so we all love going to the games in our special Red Wings jerseys, of course. Go Wings!

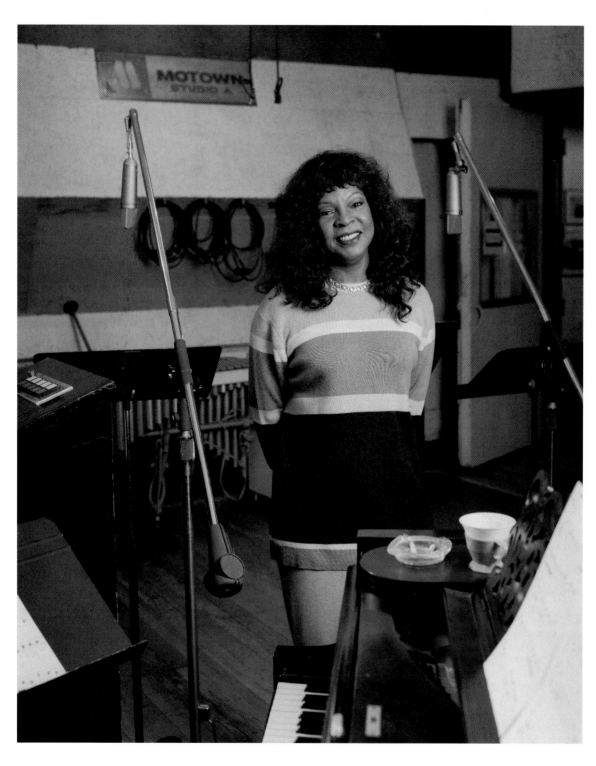

Martha Reeves is a singer and author.
Photographed at Studio A, Motown Museum, in Detroit.

All my brothers and sisters sang. We're from a singing family mainly because my grandfather was a Methodist minister, and most of our childhood was spent in church. Three to four days a week. And if it wasn't choir rehearsal it was usher boys meetings or Bible study.

We lived on Riopelle and Leland. My dad ran a tight ship; you didn't make noise in his house after a certain time and you certainly didn't come in after 12. So when I started singing in clubs, even though I was 19, I still had to be in this house by 12. I was singing during happy hour at 20 Grand, at Fourteenth and Warren. Happy hour at a night club is between three and seven. The place is now defunct, but every artist who ever played Detroit played the 20 Grand. From Ella Fitzgerald to Chuck Jackson to Billy Stewart to Lena Horne, I've seen all these people there. I think I was making five dollars a night when William Stevenson from the A-and-R Department at Motown Records discovered me. He approached me after my song, and said, "You've got talent; I want you to come to this company," and gave me a card that said "Hitsville USA." I took it lightly, 'cause I thought he was coming to hit on me — he was a good-looking man. But when I looked at the card, I realized this is where Mary Wells was from. She had a hit record at the time called "Bye Bye Baby." The story was that she had approached Berry Gordy and asked him to listen to her song that she had written. And he said, "Instead of you just giving me this song, I want you to be an artist." And he recorded her at the age of 15.

Also at that time, Marv Johnson had a record out called "You've Got What It Takes," the Miracles had a record out called "Shop Around" and the Marvelettes had a record out called "Mr. Postman." All these records were being played on the radio almost every other minute, and everybody was talking about this man, Berry Gordy. Well, I realized after receiving that card that this was the company! So I didn't go to work the next day — I worked at the cleaners — I went straight to Motown. I asked my dad how to get there on the bus. When I approached William Stevenson, he said, "What are you doing here?" I said, "Don't you remember giving me your card last night and asking me to come to this company?" He said, "Yeah, but you're supposed to take that card and set up an appointment for an audition — we have auditions every third Thursday. Tell you what. Answer this telephone. I'll be right back."

So I started answering the telephone, "This is Martha Reeves, A-and-R Department." I had a commercial course through school, so I knew the proper way to answer a phone. I was told by people that they wanted to talk to Mickey, not William Stevenson, and there was no A-and-R secretary. I said, "His name is William Stevenson, and yes, there is an A-and-R secretary, I'm Martha Reeves, and may I help you?" So I had that battle for about three hours. I was confronted by musicians — I mean angry musicians, insisting on getting paid for sessions that they had already done because there was no woman in there or anybody taking records. Nobody was writing down what songs were being recorded, nobody was writing down what musicians had spent time recording the sessions, and nobody was following through with the payroll. I straightened all that up in a matter of hours. I made a session note, I called the finance department and had this confrontation with a lady named Louise Williams who said, "There's no A-and-R Department, and who are you?" So I fixed her. I put her directly on the phone with musicians who said "We want our m' and f'in money, right now, or we're not going to cut this session." She didn't like me for that, but she said, "I'll cut them a check, it will be ready for them when they finish," and things continued. Everybody that came through the door, I dealt with. I dealt with the writers, I dealt with the musicians, and when William Stevenson came back, I was indispensable. He asked me to stay the rest of the day.

While I was working as secretary that first week, Stevie Wonder was brought to the studio. Robert White had seen this young kid, he said he was blind. But I don't ever consider Stevie Wonder as being blind, I just figure he's visually impaired — he could see better than a lot of people. He was nine years old, and he was a little mischievous. He would get into everything; you'd have to watch to keep him from getting in somebody's way, because he was curious. Whenever the studio wasn't busy with recordings, I was allowed to take him in there. I was amazed at his talent; he could play every instrument in the studio.

Berry had chosen William Stevenson and Clarence Paul as his assistants, and they're the ones who are responsible for all the talent to be gathered from Detroit. They found all the best of the jazz musicians, all the best of the amateur show winners — such as myself — and corralled them all into that one building, at 2648 West Grand Boulevard. I'm very proud of the fact that I didn't go there seeking to be discovered; I was asked there — and upon arrival, I made a place for myself.

I had quite a time. People were always there making some kind of music, because Berry owned the building. It wasn't like a business that opened at nine and closed at five — it was open 24 hours. Any time you were out at night, say for instance we went to the 20 Grand to perform or to see another act perform, we could go by Hitsville USA, and there would be some music being made. There'd be somebody either mixing, or somebody actually putting their vocals on, or some musician tidying up a track, or something. There was always some music going on at Hitsville USA.

So when people call me legendary, it doesn't offend me, because it lets me know that I was there. I am one of the ones — I'm one of the survivors. I have been supported by a record company. I have been able to withstand, not only because of the training that my mom gave me to be an individual and stand on my own but also the fact that Motown made artists, developed them and sent them on their way. Being from the Motown family is an honor in itself. Everybody worked really hard to succeed at what they do. So we got the best of everything. We got the best female vocalists, we got the best female group, the best male group, the best single performers. Everything came from Motown, and everybody had a turn to be the best.

"

I have been able to withstand, not only because

of the training that my mom gave me to be an individual

and stand on my own but also the fact that Motown made artists,

developed them and sent them on their way.

"

Bo Schembechler is a retired college football coach.

Coaching is a job of passion. You've got to love it or you'll never make it, because it's so consuming. It's a seven-day-a-week job, and it's hard. Now that I've retired, I miss the staff meetings, the player meetings, the practices, the scrimmages — the game. Really, the game. I love coaching the game. That part of it I'll miss when the season comes around — I miss that today. I don't miss recruiting, I don't miss the alumni functions, I don't miss the constant scrutiny of the media. I don't miss any of that. But the players, the coaches — that's different. That's what it's really all about.

I came to Michigan in 1969, which makes this year my 30th anniversary here. So from '69 to '99, there are 21 years of players who have played for me. This May 21, we're having our second reunion — we have them every 10 years — where everyone who played for me comes into town for a banquet at Crisler Arena.

The last banquet was a decade ago; 400 guys showed up. They had set up a head table at the east end, and then down on the floor you had tables; they catered the dinner and it was a ball. For each team that played, the captain would get up and talk. Dan Dierdorf and Jim Brandstatter were the MCs; they're two witty guys. So it was really funny — the captains would get up to the dais and start talking and pretty soon, Dierdorf or Brandstatter would come on and say, "That's enough, after five minutes we're sick of you!" So the next guy would get up and so on and so forth.

Our 1984 team had the worst record of any team we had. All through the night, they pumped that '84 team to death. Dierdorf said, "Before we start, there's one disgraceful bunch here that we probably shouldn't even have in this room. Really, I want to put it to a vote here, whether we should keep this damned '84 team in here or not." So the captain of the '84 team gets up, Doug James from Louisville, Kentucky. His nickname was "Kentucky Fried James." He played the offensive line, and he is a colorful guy, very witty. He gets up and says, "I'm tired of everybody cutting down our team. I want to tell you guys one thing. We may not have had a great year that year, but let me tell you, we led the United States of America in attendance." Which we did every year, so what's the difference?

That banquet lasted until after midnight, but nobody thought it was long.

This year it'll be a wingding, I promise you. There'll be guys who show up on May 21 who haven't been around for decades, but it'll be like they were never gone. They will be laughing, cutting on each other, crying — it's emotional. You know why? Because we knew each other so well. The one thing football does is bare your soul. You know who's tough, you know who works, you know who you can count on. Football will bring all those attributes out. If you've got any weaknesses, we know it — that's the difference. You can work with somebody at an office, and they go home at night — you don't really know them. But we get in tight battles where we need guys who've got to deliver. Some can do it, some can't. That's what football is about. If it were all physical, or all mental, it would be different. But it's both.

You have to get close with all of the players — you've got to understand the 120th guy. He's an important guy. If he doesn't have a good attitude, if he doesn't believe in the program, if he doesn't see that his playing on the demonstration team is helping us win, you're going to have a problem. Some of the great kids we've had here were big enough and strong enough not to get hurt, but not strong enough to play. Still, they made a great contribution to the program, and I'm really close with many of them to this day. Some of those guys, who were willing to be part of something that they thought was good, become enormous successes after they leave. They take the attitude with them. Like Dave Branden, who is on the Board of Regents here and was CEO of Valassis Inserts until he retired. He was a third-team guy. During a reunion of one of the teams he played on, the players were all getting up and telling the group what they were doing. So Branden got up and said, "I want you to know, when I came to Michigan I had all these visions of being starting quarterback and having a successful career here; I knew everything was going to be great for me, and I end up being moved to defensive end playing third team all the time I'm here. You know what I think, guys? I made up my mind I'm going to make a contribution to the program. I'm going to learn what goes on here, and I'm going to get something out of playing football here. And I did. And do you know what? Goddammit, I made All American in business!" And he's a multi-millionaire, so I guess he did.

At the office today I'll answer the phone until probably three or four in the afternoon — and at least three of those calls will be ex-players. Some call just to talk, some have a problem, but once you play here, you're part of the family. I hear from most of the guys who played here — and that's the great enjoyment. It keeps you going; you make so many friends that you coached and you coached with. Michigan football is a kind of an era. Wherever a guy ends up, in Tennessee or California or wherever he goes, he played football at Michigan. People will ask, "Who'd you play for?" "I played for Bo." "What's he like?" That's what they all ask … *"What's he like?"* It sets this group apart, because they're part of the Michigan football program. It's just the way it is here. They're proud of their accomplishments; that's the reason they'll come back. And that's the way it should be; that's what it's all about.

The nice thing is that when I look back on my career at Michigan, there are a lot of things I would have done differently, I second-guess myself on some things. But by and large, I have no regrets. I look back and say, if I were to figure my life for what I want to do, I did it. That's the way I feel. I did what I wanted to do. Now how many people can really say that?

"

The one thing football does is bare your soul.
You know who's tough, you know who works,
you know who you can count on.

"

Harvey Ovshinsky is a teacher, writer, producer and director.
Photographed at the Grosse Pointe Academy in Grosse Pointe.

I ask questions for a living; most documentary directors do. We ask the questions, then we stand back and we watch. And wait for the answers. We remove ourselves from the action and let the characters in our films tell their stories.

Their stories.

Not ours.

That's one reason why, for the last 15 years, I wake up most mornings at 5:30 a.m. to write stories of my own.

My stories. Not theirs.

Greenlight Gardens is the title of my latest screenplay. But this particular script is more than a movie; it has also evolved into a story about my own origins as a storyteller. And it also says something about my passion for the city I call home.

Much of *Greenlight Gardens* was inspired by my own childhood growing up on Forrer Avenue, in northwest Detroit, near Seven Mile and Greenfield. In the story, Sarah Doner is a lonely girl who desperately wants only to find her father who is missing in action in Vietnam. She finds unexpected help from the Keyman, an old, mysterious, seemingly crazy black man who is the legend of her street. What Sarah doesn't know is that before he became the Keyman, her new friend was once a brilliant, but reclusive Langston Hughes/J.D. Salinger type poet and author.

Greenlight Gardens is the name Sarah ultimately gives to the Keyman's enormous yard, which is filled with junk — large appliance parts, discarded motors and engines and other found objects. But what really attracts Sarah to the place is the "Pride of Detroit," an old biplane made of junk that the Keyman once built for his son. Eventually, the Keyman teaches Sarah and her best buddy, Danny, how to use the Pride to travel anywhere in the world, using only their own imaginations and the Keyman's magical, mysterious "flying words."

But it's not an easy process. Writing often isn't. There is much work to be done before the old man and Sarah can, as pilots like to say before taking off, make "contact." First, they both have to make sure it's safe, that there is nothing blocking their path on the runway. One of the first images Sarah and Danny were struck by in the Keyman's backyard was an old traffic light with all three lights smashed out. The first thing Sarah, Danny and the Keyman do when they start connecting with each other is replace the broken bulbs with three new ones, all green.

For each of these characters, it's time to stop being cautious. It's time to stop being stopped.

It's time to go.

I'm a real fan of go. Getting there is OK, but it's not my favorite part. It's the going that gets me out of bed every morning.

It's no accident that Sarah's turf, the geography of her neighborhood, is identical to my own growing up on Forrer.

One of my earliest memories is, as a child, seeing a Keyman-type character riding around with his three-wheeled cart, ringing his bell and shouting out invitations to sharpen scissors and knives and, of course, to make keys.

I also remember a mysterious house at the corner of our street. My father used to warn me, "Don't ever go there. Whatever you do, don't ever go there." He was never clear about why exactly we shouldn't go there. But, of course, when your parents tell you not to go somewhere, that's the first place you want to go on Saturdays when you wake up and they're sleeping in. Most neighborhoods have their own particular legends, places our parents tell us not to go. For example, if you were a child growing up on the east side of Detroit, near Mack and Mt. Elliott, your parents would be sure to say, "Don't go to Heidelberg. Don't go near Tyree Guyton. Whatever you do, don't go there." Tyree Guyton is the Keyman of his time.

My best friend, Bobby Hagopian, lived on the other side of my house. Bobby's grandparents started Hagopian and Sons Carpet Cleaning and we had marvelous adventures playing in the sheds and fields behind the original Hagopian's factory on Eight Mile.

Bobby and I shared a mutual love for monster and horror movies and science fiction films. We used to cut out and collect the newspaper ads from our all-time favorites. *It Came From Beneath the Sea, Attack of the Giant Crab Monsters, Seventh Voyage of Sinbad.* Eventually, we also started a newsletter called the *Transylvanian Newsletter,* a mimeographed fan-zine.

I wrote my heart out when I was young. Stories, poems, essays — anything with a beginning, middle and an end. When I was Sarah's and Danny's age, I started neighborhood clubs, like the Creative Boys Club. Not because I wanted to have a club, which was important, but mainly because I wanted to write and publish a newsletter of my own. In those days, I took every opportunity to just spill the beans, to write. To tell.

To go.

In *Greenlight Gardens,* there's a pivotal scene where the Keyman teaches Sarah how to find her own "flying words." He gives her several keys, each one a different size, shape and weight. He asks her to "listen" to the keys and describe each one in as much detail as possible. "Find the words," he says. "Tell me something I didn't know I didn't know."

"Don't stop, go further."

With the right "flying words" any child can become master of his own universe.

His universe, not theirs.

But you have to have the right fuel. One of the lessons I pass on to my students is the need for writers of all ages to scratch the surface. There's not much very exciting going on above the surface, nothing new, no surprises. Everything is so obvious. What you see is what you get. But below the surface, out of sight, buried deep inside and hidden from view is what I call "the good stuff." It's whatever we're thinking and feeling at the time. It's what scares us and excites us, and moves and motivates us. It's what keeps us up at night. It's everything that is closest and dearest to our hearts and souls. It's our innermost feelings, our core values. Our point of view, our essence.

It's who we are and what makes each of us tick. The good stuff is whatever matters. It's whatever counts.

And most of us can only get there by scratching the surface.

When you live in Detroit, attacking the surface can become a full-time profession. Or, if you're like me, an obsession. This city doesn't give anyone a break. It's almost impossible to penetrate. Too fortified and protected.

Too many walls, too many barriers.

Too much surface.

This city is like a difficult poem that's open for interpretation. And I only know one way in. To paraphrase Robert Frost, sometimes "the only way around is through."

I often tell my students that in poetry, the writer does fifty percent of the work and the reader must do the rest. You have to fill in the blanks. You have to read between the lines.

And you have to bring something to the table. That's important, too. The great American painter and teacher Robert Henri used to teach his students, "A good model does not unfold herself to you. You must rise to meet her."

It's the same with Detroit. This isn't New York, or Toronto, or Seattle. In this town, nobody gives you a break, you have to do all the work. If you want access, if you want in, you have to be your own artist, your own poet.

Your own Keyman.

If you want to truly enjoy this city and discover all its hidden surprises, you can't knock and hope somebody answers. You have to "rise to meet her." You have to look beyond the surface to find out what's going on below. You have to dig. You have to search.

You have to scratch.

Otherwise you're either going to be a stranger in your own hometown or you're going to be bored silly. You won't know where to go or what to do with your energy. You'll just stay put, stuck, removed, aloof. On automatic pilot. Like Sarah and Danny, and the Keyman before they made contact and found each other. Forever coasting and gliding above the surface.

And going nowhere. Fast.

And along the way, missing out on an awful lot of the good stuff.

Ken Mikolowski is a poet; Ann Mikolowski was an artist.
Together they founded The Alternative Press.
Photographed at their home/studio in Ann Arbor.

First of all we were a community: a community of artists, writers, musicians, politicos and others. We mostly lived in an area of Detroit known as the Cass Corridor. We lived there at the time *Newsweek* magazine did a cover story entitled *"What Is Wrong With America's Cities?"* and listed Detroit as not only the worst city in the country, but among the worst cities in the history of the world. It was compared to Shanghai of old, and Sodom and Gomorrah. For those of us who lived there at the time this was pure macho delight. We lived in *"one of the worst places in the history of the world"* and we were survivors, but more than that we reveled in it, and we swaggered when we walked. We didn't own much, but we owned this, and we made art of it.

The music of the MC5, Iggy and the Stooges, Mitch Ryder and the Detroit Wheels reflected this gritty, urban funk. And artists Gordon Newton, Bob Sestok, Brenda Goodman, Michael and Kathryn Luchs, Paul Schwarz, Ellen Phelan, Bradley Jones, Nancy Pletos, Jim Chatelain and many more showed the art of our community in our cooperative gallery, the Willis, in the heart of the Cass Corridor. Poets like Jim Gustafson, Faye Kicknosway, Andrei Codrescu, Mick Vranich, John Sinclair and Donna Brook read their poems at the Willis Gallery, often accompanied by bands like the Shadowfax or Bobby MacDonald. We were a community doing our art in our community.

In 1969, Ann and I moved a big old letterpress from the Artists Workshop into the basement of our home on Avery Street. We had never printed before in our lives, but we had this desire to combine our talents as artist and poet into something called *The Alternative Press*, so we could publish this new work of our friends, our community. It was and remains a labor of love, with the accent strongly on the labor part. Everything we've printed for the past 30 years has been with hand-set type and paper placed one sheet at a time into a press remarkably like the first one used by Gutenberg. But that's always been the aesthetic of Cass Corridor art — to use the materials at hand (whatever you have) and make art of it.

Artists would frequently gather around our kitchen table and make art (usually on postcards printed on the press) and trade their works with our son Michael who was working alongside them. And often out-of-town poets like Robert Creeley, Diane di Prima, Allen Ginsberg or Anne Waldman would stay at our house when they gave readings in the city and then leave poems for us to print on our press in the basement. There were many of these outside sources of inspiration, but in the main we were greatly influenced by each other: poets, artists and musicians of Detroit feeding each other energy, a creative spirit we still feel today. Ann continues to make art and I still write poems and together we will run *The Alternative Press*, but it's in another time and in another place.

David DiChiera is the founder of Michigan Opera Theater.
Photographed at Detroit Opera House in Detroit.

In the early seventies I left my position as a tenured professor at Oakland University to embark upon my quest to build an opera company for Detroit. Having just reopened the Music Hall as a performing arts center and home for Michigan Opera Theatre after years of neglect, I was driven to convert everyone in my path into an opera lover. Well, maybe not *everyone* — not someone like Walter.

Walter Briggs was the grandson of W. O. Briggs of Briggs Stadium fame (later renamed Tiger Stadium). His wife, Gwen, and my wife, Karen, had been friends since childhood, so we knew each other socially but weren't exactly buddies. He had always made it clear to me that he had no interest in opera and that we had little in common. For my part, I had only marginal interest in sports then.

Our wives had tried to get Walter and me to become closer, but they had little success. For instance, when Gwen suggested that we play tennis together, Walter objected, "But David's a *musician*." Finally, one evening as the four of us dined, Karen had an idea: "Walter has never been to an opera and David has never been to a football game. Let's get them to host one another." We were both up to the challenge; Walter said he would see the current production at Music Hall, and I agreed to attend the Lions' Thanksgiving Day game at Tiger Stadium.

I was first to serve as host. Walter came down to see our production of Menotti's *The Medium*. To stir the first-timer's interest, I mentioned that Sal Mineo would be starring in it. I learned only later how much consternation that bit of information caused him. Walter could not figure out what the famous actor was doing in an opera. When he got to Music Hall, though, he was relieved to learn that Sal Mineo wasn't there to sing, but to act, since his role was that of the mute gypsy, Toby.

Next, it was my turn to be Walter's nervous guest. Not only had I never been to a football game, I had never been to a professional sports stadium of any kind. Not the least of my worries was figuring out what to wear. In those days the Lions played at Tiger Stadium, and though I had never been there, I was painfully aware that it was out-of-doors.

I was *terrified* of the cold. When I moved here from southern California I went to the army surplus store and bought the biggest, heaviest parka on the rack. It had zippers, snaps and buckles and fur spilling out of the hood and sleeves. When I put it on, it was so thick that my arms wouldn't hang naturally at my sides — they just sort of stuck out like the arms of an infant bundled up by a protective mother.

The parka was warm, but with all the soft fur, I figured it wasn't appropriate for viewing football. "Me and some guys" were going to the Lions' game, in a van. Football, I had always imagined, was a savage sport played on frozen tundra. Even in the dead of winter, some Detroit fans

wore nothing above the waist but blue and silver paint.
I went to the ski shop and bought a suave, but manly,
lightweight ski jacket.

Thanksgiving Day arrived; I spent the greater part of the
morning in front of a mirror convincing myself that my
chosen attire was football worthy. Walter Briggs arrived at
my door covered, from head to toe, in fur. He wore an ankle-
length raccoon coat, fur hat and gloves. I think he even
had fur boots.

It was bitter cold at the stadium, but I enjoyed the V.I.P.
treatment that the Briggs name allowed. It being my first
game, I needed coaching. I continually asked questions
such as, "Why did they move the ball back three feet?"

Everyone near listened with amusement as Walter gave this
grown man a play-by-play explanation. Joe Namath was
on the field — the only name I recognized. He ran about
taking bows like an opera prima donna. I all but froze in
my suave but manly ski jacket; my host reached into his
raccoon coat and passed me a flask.

Walter became my friend that November day at Tiger
Stadium. Not long after, he moved to New York; the
Lions went to Pontiac and my opera company left Music
Hall. Briggs is now a committed theater-goer back east.
I was sorry to lose him from Detroit, but I enjoyed my
newfound friendship.

"

Football, I had always imagined,

was a savage sport played on frozen tundra.

Even in the dead of winter, some Detroit fans wore nothing

above the waist but blue and silver paint.

"

Jimmy Schmidt is a noted American chef.
Photographed at The Rattlesnake Club in Detroit.

When I opened the Rattlesnake Club, I chose Detroit partly because my wife is from here, but also because I truly believe in the future of this city.

I wanted the restaurant to be by the river, because in addition to liking the water, I saw the river as the lifeline to the city. Shopping around for a building, we found this one in the Stroh River Place complex. It's actually shaped by the river; it's an equilateral parallelogram. The original lot lines were drawn parallel to the river, and since the river is crooked, so is the building. If you look up into the coffers of the ceiling, you'll notice by the way the 12-inch by 12-inch acoustic tiles fit together how dramatic the angles are. It's an Albert Kahn building, very artistic, which fit my vision for the restaurant. I wanted the whole dining environment to be artistic. From Georg Jensen silverware to the Saarinen furniture from the Cranbrook School, to the collection of modern art and the background music.

When we opened in June of 1988, we planned a big opening week, including a large private party we'd invited from *Bon Appetit* magazine. That particular evening turned out to be right in the middle of a heat wave. To make it even more interesting, at the time we opened, all the ancillary support areas were being redone, including the roads. The streets

had all been dug out. Fortunately, our guests were very strong-willed. However, our food-delivery service was not. When the trucks got to our block, they saw the roads weren't there and just turned around and left. So on the night of this big event, when we finally figured out the trucks weren't coming, there we were, running out to the market, scrambling for supplies. That set us behind schedule from the start.

For the first course I had planned chilled artichoke soup. We basically started cooking the artichokes just half an hour before the party started. And artichokes take half an hour to cook. The next step was to puree them, and we were still doing that when the guests began to arrive. Then, the soup still had to be chilled — it was a hot night, remember. I had to get inventive fast, so I proceeded to run the artichoke soup through our ice cream machine. It chilled the soup in about six minutes — it worked great. The publisher of *Bon Appetit* commented, "Your soup tasted so fresh!" I thought to myself, *You don't know the half of it.*

Al Kaline is a television broadcaster
and former Detroit Tigers player.
Photographed at Tiger Stadium in Detroit.

I signed with Detroit Tigers right out of high school. I graduated on June 18, 1953, and I joined the ball club on June 20. My father and I took a train to Philadelphia — the Tigers were playing the Phillies — along with the scout that signed me — a guy from Pennsylvania named Ed Catalinas, who eventually became head of the scouting bureau for the Tigers and also a good friend of mine. The Tigers' manager, Fred Hutchinson, was a very burly guy, a really angry-looking guy. He was actually a gentle person, but as a skinny 18-year-old kid, I was scared to death of him. In Philadelphia, he put me in the first game. He didn't even know my name; he just said, "Hey, kid, get a bat and pinch hit." It was about the eighth inning. I didn't have a bat, so I just grabbed the first one I could find, and it was too big for me, too heavy. I hit the first pitch to center field for an out, but I was so happy to get out of there and get back to the dugout where I belonged at that time. After that game we went to St. Louis, then we took a train home to Detroit. Back in those days we always traveled by train. We got in about four in the morning, and as we were coming into the train station, I was sitting next to a veteran player named Johnny Pesky. He said, "Hey, kid, look over there — that's your home for the next few years. It looks like an old battleship." And sure enough, going by Michigan Avenue you could see what we called Briggs Stadium at that time, and it looked like a big aircraft carrier.

That night, I went to the Tuller Hotel on Grand Circus Park, which is where I lived for the first six months. Several of the players were staying there. I didn't know where to go, so they said, "Come with us, you can stay at the Tuller." It was very cheap; at that time I think it was $5 a day. It still added up to a lot of money when you had to pay every day. Those hotels made it convenient for us, though — we could keep our clothes in the room while we were on the road, and they didn't charge us. That was nice, because we didn't have to pack up our clothes all the time and put them in suitcases.

The next day we had a game, so I walked out of the hotel and headed down Michigan Avenue. We could walk there from the hotel; it wasn't that far from downtown to Briggs Stadium. I remember trying to find my way into the stadium — I didn't know which way to go, or how to get to the locker room, because I'd never been there before. The police stopped me at one point, and they didn't believe me when I told them who I was. I had to show my identification because I didn't look like I should have been a major league ballplayer. I finally got in. And the first thing I did, before I went into the locker room, was walk into the stands and take a look at the field. God, it was beautiful. All the seats were green at that time; the field was as green as you could possibly see it. I'll never forget that day.

I'll be starting my 46th year with the Tigers. The last day at old Tiger Stadium is going to be emotional for me, because that's the only job I've ever gone to every summer. The new stadium will be good for the city, but it will be hard to duplicate the closeness you feel in the old stadium. With no posts, the upper deck will have to seated way back from the field. I love this town, especially in summertime. I'd never move anyplace else. After all these years, I still have a good job with the Tigers. Life is good.

Philip Levine is a poet.
Photographed at Washington Square, New York City, New York.

SMOKE

Can you imagine the air filled with smoke?
It was. The city was vanishing before noon
or was it earlier than that? I can't say because
the light came from nowhere and went nowhere.

This was years ago, before you were born, before
your parents met in a bus station downtown.
She'd come on Friday after work all the way
from Toledo, and he'd dressed in his only suit.

Back then we called this a date, sometimes
a blind date, though they'd written back and forth
for weeks. What actually took place is now lost.
It's become part of the mythology of a family,

the stories told by children around the dinner table.
No, they aren't dead, they're just treated that way,
as objects turned one way and then another
to catch the light, the light overflowing with smoke.

Go back to the beginning, you insist. Why
is the air filled with smoke? Simple. We had work.
Work was something that thrived on fire, that without
fire couldn't catch its breath or hang on for life.

We came out into the morning air, Bernie, Stash,
Williams, and I, it was late March, a new war
was starting up in Asia or closer to home,
one that meant to kill us, but for a moment

the air held still in the gray poplars and elms
undoing their branches. I understood the moon
for the very first time, why it came and went, why
it wasn't there that day to greet the four of us.

Before the bus came a small, black bird settled
on the curb, fearless or hurt, and turned its beak up
as though questioning the day. "A baby crow,"
someone said. Your father knelt down on the wet cement,

his lunchbox balanced on one knee and stared quietly
for a long time. "A grackle far from home," he said.
One of the four of us mentioned tenderness,
a word I wasn't used to, so it wasn't me.

The bus must have arrived. I'm not there today.
The windows were soiled. We swayed this way and that
over the railroad tracks, across Woodward Avenue,
heading west, just like the sun, hidden in smoke.

Christine Lahti is an actress and director.
Photographed at her home in Santa Monica, California.

As a kid growing up in Royal Oak and later, Birmingham, I was always acting. Just about any chance I got, I'd figure out ways to put on a performance. In our basement in Birmingham, my girlfriends in the neighborhood would come over and we'd set up a stage, complete with a curtain, which we made out of a rope and a sheet.

Musicals were our specialty — we did a great rendition of "I'm Gonna Wash that Man Right Out of My Hair" from *South Pacific.* That was one of our biggest numbers. Our repertoire included a variety of things; we'd either put on albums and pantomime along with them, or do our own karaoke situation, where we'd sing and act out the songs. Sometimes we did duets, sometimes we did solos, and sometimes we performed as a whole group.

And what performance would be complete without an audience? We invited people around the neighborhood, so usually the neighborhood kids would come, and sometimes we'd get the parents to come. I don't think we charged admission — if we did, at the most we charged a dime. That was a lot of fun to do — a great activity for a bunch of eight-year-olds.

When I wasn't putting on performances with my friends, I was going to see them with my parents. They would take my brothers and sisters and I downtown to see plays and musicals at the Fisher Theatre, and they'd also take us downtown to see the big movies, like *Ben Hur, Spartacus* and *The Ten Commandments.* There was nothing like seeing those movies in the big old theaters in Detroit. There were six kids in our family, including me, and we all looked forward to our trips downtown.

I'll never forget the very first time we went to the Fisher Theatre — we saw *Hello Dolly,* with Carol Channing. That was a real milestone to me. I had never seen or heard a live musical; in fact, it was the first time I had seen any live production at all. The theater experience was brand new to me, and I loved every minute of it. I was inspired from the moment we walked into the theater, which felt so big and grand. I thought Carol Channing was wonderful and funny, of course, and the costumes were really gorgeous — especially the scene with all the hats. I loved those ornate, beautiful hats.

Growing up in the Detroit area inspired me in many different ways; I am so glad my parents gave us the opportunity to see those films, plays and musicals as kids. I know that having exposure at an early age to those great performers had a direct influence on me.

Dick Purtan is a radio personality.
Photographed at Hart Plaza in Detroit.

I grew up in Kenmore, which is a suburb of Buffalo, New York. My dad was in sales to the furniture business; he sold anything to do with furniture, like vinyl, plastic, cotton, springs, leather. (He still is, by the way; he's 88 years old and has his own rep firm.) At the time, Detroit was part of his territory, and in the summers, when I was still in grammar school, my mother and I would go along on his business trips to Detroit. And rather than driving, flying or going by train, we used to come here on the D&C Lines, which were the boat lines. We would take the *City of Detroit* boat from Buffalo, to Cleveland, to Detroit.

I remember the ship looked like a fancy Boblo boat. You could actually take your car onto it, and there were cabins — staterooms where you could sleep for the night. So in Buffalo we would drive our car right onto the bottom deck of the boat, park, and then head to the upper deck, which was for passengers. Then the boat would go to Cleveland, and on to Detroit, and it would tie up right at the foot of Woodward Avenue, where we'd drive off. The trip took two days. Then, when the boat returned to Detroit, we'd get back on the ship, and sail to Cleveland and back to Buffalo.

Because of those trips as a kid, I got to know Detroit pretty well. We stayed at the Statler Hotel, which was on Woodward right at Grand Circus Park. Across Woodward from the Statler was a place called the Adams Grill, where we would eat breakfast. Then, while my dad was making sales calls, my mom and I went to movies, went shopping at Hudson's downtown and visited Greenfield Village. In the evenings, we would very often have dinner at the Roma Café in the Eastern Market. I'd always order spaghetti. I loved it then as I love it now (then we called it spaghetti, now we call it pasta). We ate there so much, in fact, that I got to know the owner, Hector Sossi. Hector grew up in Cleveland, and he was named after his next-door neighbor, Hector Boiardi — or as we know him, Chef Boyardee.

Old habits die hard. My wife, Gail, and I still eat at the Roma Café quite a bit. One winter back in the middle to late '70s, when I was at WXYZ Radio (now WXYT), I decided that we should have dinner one more time at the Statler Hotel. The hotel had been closed for some time, but we had a contest and invited 30 or 40 listeners to meet there for dinner. We made arrangements to get into one of the banquet rooms; there was no heat and no light. We had food catered from the Roma — my wife and I and some friends picked it up and brought over in our station wagon. We served it hot and had tables set up with candles. We even brought in a four-piece chamber music group from the Detroit Symphony Orchestra. They played while we enjoyed dinner with pasta, veal, chicken and wine, sitting there in our coats, hats and gloves.

So it all started with my mom and dad (as it always does) … my dad's love of boats and his business trips to Detroit. I decided I wanted to work in Detroit because I already knew the town. I knew the streets, the department stores, I had a feel for it. In 1965 I was working in Cincinnati when I heard there was a job opening here, at WKNR, Keener 13. I called and sent an audition tape to see if I could get a job, and they hired me. May 24, 1965 was the day I started; I did the 10 p.m. to 1 a.m. show for two months, and they decided instead of that I should be doing mornings, and I've been doing mornings ever since. I've been getting up at three and four in the morning for a lot of years now — a lot of good years.

Gordie Howe is a legendary hockey player.

Colleen Howe is an author, producer, mother of five children and grandmother of nine grandchildren.

Photographed at Thunderbird Lanes in Troy.

Gordie:

Ma Shaw was the grand old lady of the Red Wings hockey team. That's where I stayed when I first played — she owned a house that was right near Olympia, along with Ted Lindsay, Metro Prystai, Marty Pavelich and Red Kelly. Before we lived there, her place housed the likes of Quackenbush and Stewart and Lumley and the heavy hitters. It was convenient, because you could wake up only half an hour before you were supposed to be at the Olympia, get dressed and you're there.

Ted, Marty, Red and I, being young, were the four kids who had to go to everything — banquets, events and other things for the team. Jack Adams would come into the room and say, "We need volunteers to go to such-and-such a banquet," and they always said, "Ted, Red, Gordie and Marty." So we went. I was alone a lot with those kids. Being young individuals who didn't have enough money to do much of anything, we didn't mind. When we weren't going to banquets, Vic Stasiuk and I used to go to the Lucky Strike bowling alley; it was only about a one-and-a-half blocks from the Olympia. We bowled quite a bit in those days.

One night, at the Lucky Strike, I saw this very attractive young blonde. She was wearing a pair of blue jeans, which she made quite fashionable. And when I saw her I was at a point where it was better to watch her than bowl myself, so that's what I did. I used to go up and watch her bowl, and I became the original stalker. I found out what time she bowled and showed up to watch. She was usually with this elderly gentleman; it was her stepfather, Budd, although I didn't know it at the time.

— continued on next page

Colleen:

It was 1950, and all that was on my mind were my friends in high school, being president of the modern dance class, and making some various income through the cooperative retailing program offered by the Detroit Board of Education. There was never a dull moment. I was on top of the world. I was going to rule the world. I was going to be in charge of General Motors building. At least in my mind, that's what I was going to do. I always had these dreams of being a person who could really make things happen. Little wonder that I never paid much attention to my father who was up in arms about a famous hockey player named Gordie Howe who suffered a serious injury the night before at the Red Wings game. "See ya, Dad," was what I said, because I had to jump over the fence and get to Mackenzie High School. All my prior years I had gone to Northwestern High. I bolted out the door, unknowing that the man I would meet and marry was gravely injured and the world of hockey was praying for him to survive. It was many months later when fate had some surprises in store for Gordie and for me.

My father had meant a lot to me and, being from Toledo, he taught me to bowl. We bowled once a week together at the Lucky Strike bowling alley, right across from Northwestern High School, on Grand River and West Grand Boulevard.

Gordie had showed up many nights to watch me bowl. Gordie was always a very shy person, not one to flaunt his popularity. The night he approached me, I can remember vividly what he had on — a beautiful suede jacket he had bought when he was in his home town of Saskatoon. He said, "Hi, my name is Gordie." That was his line. "I've been

— continued on next page

Gordie:

I waited and talked to some of the people around the bowling alley and finally found someone who knew her and could give me an introduction. I just didn't want to go up on a wing and a prayer and say, "Hi, I'm so-and-so." I figured that wouldn't go very far. So I finally met her and we enjoyed each other. I asked her if I could drive her home, but she had her dad's car, so she said she couldn't do that. Then, I got enough guts to ask someone for her phone number. When I did, that let me call her. We had a steady conversation from that point out.

I finally got enough nerve to take her out. We went out for dinner, and then went to Jeff Seller's, a bar/restaurant straight out Grand River towards Oakman Boulevard. What I didn't know was that her mom and dad owned a bar on Grand River, closer to the Olympia, and Jeff knew Colleen very well. They knew she and I were underage, but the guys used to take me in there. A fella sat next to me and asked, "Are you having a beer?" I said, "No, just a Coke." He leaned forward and I saw a gun in his holster. I thought, "Oh, God, they must have sent him over to scare me." The owners came over and said hello; they didn't say anything else. We were just in there drinking our soft drinks. We had a ton of fun, but I hadn't met her parents yet. When I took her home, and went in to drop her off at the house, I saw her dad and he was not looking too friendly. I said I'd better not go in, but she said, "No, no, come on in," so I went in and she said, "Dad, I'd like you to meet ... " and he said, "I know Gordie. He's the man I told you about who got hurt in the Red Wings last season."

— continued on next page

Colleen:

watching you bowl, and maybe we could go out and have a soft drink, and I could drive you home." Of course, in those days, it was safe to have a ride home with a stranger. My heart sank, because my dad wasn't there that night, and he had let me use the car. I thought to myself, "I can't believe it — I've got the car and now this wonderful, handsome guy is asking to take me home." I couldn't leave the car there, because my mother would have a fit; she needed to get to work in the morning. All these things were going through my mind, but finally I just had to say I couldn't — and I thought I would never see him again. Would he come back?

But sure enough, Gordie got my unlisted telephone number from a friend of ours who ran the bowling alley. He started calling me, and we just talked like two teenagers would talk; I would lie on the floor with my feet resting up on the wall. When we talked, he never told me anything about himself — he just talked about his eight brothers and sisters, his mom and his dad, and what his home was like in Saskatoon.

For my cooperative retailing class, I would drive downtown and work until nine when the stores closed. That was a great place to be back then. Gordie asked if he could take me out on a date some night, and I said sure. He knew I worked late, so we went to the Michigan Theatre. About halfway through the show he reached over and touched my hand, and I almost fainted. I thought, "Oh my God, he's touching my hand!" It sounds so corny, but that's the way it was. After the show, he said, "I'd like to take you for a bite to eat afterwards, too." So he took me to a bar where Ted Lindsay and his fiancée, Pat, were that night. I knew the people

— continued on next page

Gordie:

At first I never told Colleen what I did. Maybe I wanted her to like me for who I was, and not for being a hockey player. It was different, but it's so funny because when I took her into Carl's Chop House, on Grand River, people were coming up and saying hello. She said, "My God, you know a lot of people." It was fun.

After the season ended, I had to go back home to Canada, and I told Colleen I'd be back in August. I wasn't one to sit down and write, but I decided I admired this girl and I loved her to the point where I put her picture and my picture next to each other, took a picture of the two of them together and sent that to her. She said that was the first thing I had done that showed her I really was smitten. It was a good feeling on both sides. I wanted to tell her that I did miss her and secondly, although I was a little slow with the words, the picture of the two of us together kind of hit home.

Colleen:

who owned the place. It was a nice bar/restaurant, not the kind of place where people were falling-down drunk. But I wasn't old enough to be there at that point. So the owners, Ronnie and Jeff Sellers, came up and asked me, "What are you doing in here? Do your mom and dad know you're here?"

I said, "Well, I'm not drinking or anything . . ." So they put us in a quiet corner and we just had a light dinner, but I was extremely worried that my parents would find out. As it turned out, the owners *had* called my parents, because when I got home my mother was a quite frantic. "We've really got to meet this fellow, because he's calling all the time," she said. So I brought Gordie in to meet them, and when he came in, my dad said, "Oh my gosh, you're Gordie Howe!"

My dad knew who Gordie Howe was; only *I* didn't know who Gordie Howe was! I knew his name was Gordie, but I hadn't asked his last name. And being so involved with school activities, I had never seen a hockey game.

Our life together since then has been a whirlwind. I know I've grown a lot from knowing Gordie, and I appreciate what a great dad and husband he is. I also pat myself on the back once in a while, for running the business end of our lives. We've been a perfect team.

Stewart Francke is a musician.
Photographed in Lake Orion.

Detroit rock 'n' roll. When a large group of us initially organized a series of concerts in tribute to Rob Tyner in 1992, it was both a reaction to his unexpected death and a testimonial to the way he'd lived. But it also became a lesson as to why Detroit rock is so vital, and so singularly renowned. It became something close to a passing of the torch from the '60s rockers to my own generation, if only in the sense that we learned so much about what community means from them. The original statement of purpose, written by my co-chair Ben Edmonds, read: "In 1968 Rob Tyner warned us that separation is doom. Yet that simple phrase could well hold true for our situation today. And with that phrase, Tyner, the voice of the MC5, provided us not only with a description of our problem but a key to its solution as well."

The quality of spirit behind those February 1992 shows — there were lines around the block at the State Theater — evidenced the vibrant nature of Rob's life. But it was more than just a night. People still actively talk about Rob's life and music, often recalling the feel of that night. The coalescence of various sections of Detroit's creative community — filmmakers, DJs, publicists, club owners and musicians — was a statement upon a statement: It was an affectionate and powerful reaction to another man being extravagantly alive.

A large percentage of the funds generated by the memorial concert were donated to a private scholarship fund for the education of Rob and Becky Tyner's three children. The remaining proceeds went toward establishing a scholarship in Rob's name at the Center For Creative Studies. The Rob Tyner Scholarship now stands on its own and is the principal funding target of the Detroit Music Awards.

By organizing these memorial concerts, we had hoped to make a statement larger than any dollar amount could do. In helping to remind Detroit and Detroiters of the immense natural resource that we have in the arts, we honored the spirit of our friend Rob Tyner. And we also honored ourselves. Public awareness through music is the most powerful weapon we possess in countering any threat to our community resources.

Most artists, even those working in rock and roll, are working in an attempt to add some clarification to the chaos and uncertainty that life continually presents. Tyner worked by injecting more chaos. And the music that resulted was so extravagantly alive that it drew anyone similarly alive to it.

Yet the ultimate value of Rob's life and music was in its morality. He possessed the ability, like his contemporary, Bob Seger, to comment on the "real" world while he simultaneously created a felicitous world of moral truth. After all, he always seemed to remind me, we are looking for what it is to live, more or less, from this music.

I, like many of us now making music here in Detroit, was too young to witness those tumultuous Grande Ballroom shows. And like many other people my age, I moved through rock 'n' roll backwards: The Beatles took me to Buddy Holly and the Everly Brothers, Springsteen led me to Roy Orbison, The Animals brought me to John Lee Hooker. But to hear the MC5's "Sister Anne" when I was 15 years old in a living room on a hot day in Saginaw, Michigan, when there was virtually nothing going on — there wasn't even any traffic outside — that was an explosion of possibilities that I pretty much haven't recovered from.

I moved here to Detroit partially as a result of that lingering promise. And one day, at the Shopping Center Market in Berkley, I spotted Tyner, lead singer of the MC5. Now you don't always react well when you see your teenage rock god in such banal settings, so I did what any adult would do — I hid behind the frozen foods. And I watched Rob, dressed in jeans, calf-high combat boots, a leather jacket and what could only be described as an Afro-Caucasian hair style, compare heads of lettuce. How, I thought, does Rob Tyner choose fruit or lettuce? He's gotta throw them at the wall and keep the one that doesn't explode. But he gently filled his cart. A while later, on a very hot day, I introduced myself. And this was perhaps his singular beauty: He acted as if he had known me forever. So to say that there are many who knew him longer and/or better is certainly true. But when he spoke to you, it was as if you were the only person in the room. And many rooms were crowded.

What he — and his generation: The Rationals, SRC, the MC5, the Stooges, The Woolies — leaves us in this community is, first of all, a sense of ourselves as a community. Rob both embodied and espoused an unspoken ethos: If you're a musician and you're from Detroit, there's a certain way we do things around here. It's what we sing about when we sing. It's how we wear what we wear. And it's not about just being bad, which is a common misconception. It's about forgiveness and tolerance and avoiding the chasm between artist and image. It's about leaving a part of yourself on every stage you take and never faking it. Kick out the jams, motherfucker.

I last spoke with Rob about a month before he died while researching a story on Detroit music. We spoke for quite a long time, yet he never mentioned the MC5. Instead, he talked eloquently of his love of Scott Morgan and Seger's early sides and Iggy and SRC until I asked him about all of the bands out there today that have so obviously copped the MC5's sound and moves. He paused for some time then replied, "Stewart, you can't copyright sweating."

"

How, I thought, does Rob Tyner choose fruit or lettuce?

He's gotta throw them at the wall and keep

the one that doesn't explode.

"

David Patrick Kelly is an actor.
Photographed at Old St. Patrick's Cathedral in New York City, New York.

DAVID PATRICK KELLY

This photo was taken in front of Old St. Patrick's Cathedral in lower Manhattan. The Irish Brigade left from here for the Civil War. My great-grand-uncle, Fr. William Corby, was their chaplain. He was born and raised in Detroit. His father was a landowner in Detroit and he willed some land to Fr. Corby. The land was sold and became an endowment for a French missionary school in Indiana called Notre Dame. Fr. Corby was the third president of the university.

My father's name was Robert Corby Kelly. He graduated from Eastern High School and went to work as a stockbroker in one of the art deco buildings of downtown Detroit.

The French and Irish also intertwine on my mother's side. My grandfather, Daniel Murphy, of Cork, met my grandmother, Emma Martineau, of Quebec, on the Belle Isle bridge sometime around the turn of the last century. My mother, Margaret, is one of the seven children born to them. She graduated from St. Bernard's High School and became a salesgirl at Hudson's. She and my father met on a blind date, married and had seven children, all born at St. Joseph Mercy Hospital downtown.

My father took my brother, John, and I to see John F. Kennedy speak on the steps at the old Ambassador Hotel. Eight years later, three friends and I skipped school to see Robert Kennedy speak. *Detroit Free Press* photographer Tony Spina caught us in the front rows and blew our alibi on the front page. I once played hockey with Mark Howe at Finney High School on the east side and Dave DeBusschere grew up shooting hoops on his garage net a few blocks away.

I saw The Beatles at the now-demolished Olympia Stadium and The Doors at Cobo Hall. The MC5 played at our junior dance. For a short time in college, I lived across the street from the old Motown recording studios on West Grand Boulevard. A producer there once actually offered me a songwriting contract. I told him I'd better stick to being an actor. My first union job as an actor was the lead in *Hair* for the legendary Detroit impresarios, the Nederlanders. They told me I should be in New York.

For me, Detroit will always be the city that taught me about art and music. My father was a painter, and he loved to take us to the Detroit Institute of Arts. The great mural by Diego Rivera was my favorite. My mother plays the piano, and once we were walking down Whittier past the Pied Piper Music Store, now gone, when I spied a mandolin. I don't remember asking for it, but on St. Patrick's Day in 1964, she presented it to me. I played Motown and The Beatles on it.

I loved the hydroplane races on the Detroit River, the caramel cake at Sanders, the Cadillac-Harper bus, the American and Lafayette Coney Island hot dog restaurants and Stroh's beer. I used to wear a great linen dashiki and black Beatle boots from Flagg Brothers shoe store. That was my version of Detroit style that still is a certain sound and look and feeling in my heart.

Soupy Sales is a comedian.
Photographed at the Friars Club in New York City, New York.

Detroit was a great market for live TV. I lived in Cincinnati in 1950 when I started working in television. I moved to Cleveland a year later. Then, in 1953, Stan Dale, who was a disc jockey at WXYZ, suggested I come up to audition. So I made the rounds. I went to CKLW, they said no. WJR said no. WJBK said no. But the next station I went to was WXYZ. It was a very nice operation, and I liked it. And I thought everybody was happy with me. John Lee was the program director. So I went back to Cleveland, and about two or three weeks later they called up and said John Pival, the production chief, was a huge fan of mine, he had seen me in Cincinnati. And I went and auditioned and they liked me. So that was it. I moved to Detroit in 1953 — I lived in a duplex on Schaefer and Seven Mile Road.

Of course, Detroit was the jumpingest place in the world. They had 28 clubs. We went to the Alamo, Baker's, The Crest (that was a wonderful jazz club on West Grand Boulevard), the Rouge Lounge out in River Rouge, we went to the London Chop House … it was great. Detroit was jumping. It was a great social thing there, great jazz clubs.

Every Friday night we always went to the Capitol Theatre, because they played horror movies. It was the only all-night theater in Detroit, so we'd go there and stay up all night long. We saw *Invasion of the Body Snatchers* there, and all those movies of the '50s. Then we went to the Elmwood Casino over in Windsor to see all the big acts, and we saw Marv Welch at Harry & Alma's comedy club on Gratiot.

It was a great town for sports, too. Harvey Kuenn and Al Kaline were starting with the Tigers, Gordie Howe was starting with the Red Wings, and the Lions had Bobby Layne, Bob Hoernschemeyer, Leon Hart and Joe Schmidt.

They had the great hamburger place called Biff's; there were two or three places around town. Cornings had a place on Woodward and Fourteen Mile that was open late for food.

I'd go to work at seven in the morning, do my show opposite the *Today Show*. I beat them every day, every morning. And then when I got through I'd work on the nighttime show. I did the nighttime show for seven years. I napped during the day. I was meeting myself coming and going. It really wasn't that easy, but I was about 24 years old at the time. I could take those hours then, I sure couldn't do it now.

It was great. I loved Detroit; I still do. It was wonderful.

Rabbi Charles H. Rosenzweig is founder of the Holocaust Memorial Center.
Photographed at the Holocaust Memorial Center in West Bloomfield.

RABBI CHARLES H. ROSENZVEIG

I was about 30 years old, a rabbi in Port Huron on the weekends and holidays, and teaching at the United Hebrew School in Detroit during the week. It was the evening of January 11, 1958, and I was scheduled to speak at a dinner at the Latin Quarter on Grand Boulevard and Woodward Avenue. It was an event for an organization called the Holocaust Survivors.

There were a few hundred people at the dinner; my wife and I were sitting up at the dais. I was going to talk about the importance of the survivors community keeping together — the need for all survivors to be of service to one another.

When it came time for my address, I stood up and began to speak. Suddenly, I felt my wife kick me. She had never done anything like that before, so thinking it must have been an accident, I continued to speak as though nothing had happened. Then she kicked me again, harder. And she kept kicking me. Nobody at the dinner knew what was going on, but finally I realized something urgent must be taking place. I ended the speech quickly, abruptly finishing the address, and I got off the dais right there and then. I sat down and asked my wife, "What's the matter?"

"I have to go to the hospital," my wife said. She was pregnant at the time. "You'd better take me now." We left right away. The night was cold, and it was snowing. We got into my Ford and headed, very quickly, to Sinai Hospital on Outer Drive. She gave birth an hour later to our boy, Eli. Eli is 41 now, and he has five children of his own.

I have been in Detroit since 1951, since my wife and I were married here. I had lived in New York for four years after I immigrated to the United States from Poland. As a young person, I loved the dynamics of New York, so when I flew in to Willow Run airport 48 years ago, Michigan seemed a little too quiet for me. But I got used to it, little by little, and I grew to love it here. It's been 41 years since that cold night in January when Eli was born, and we still enjoy living here, we still love the combination of strong communities and active city life, we still love Detroit's diverse cultural community.

Denise Ilitch is vice chairwoman of Little Caesar Enterprises, Inc.
Photographed at Joe Louis Arena in Detroit.

It was a sea of red and white. I will never forget the Detroit Red Wings' victory parade on June 10, 1997, just after the team won the Stanley Cup. The weather that day was absolutely beautiful. And, the excitement and anticipation of the parade was really dramatic because it was something that we had never experienced — the last time the Wings had won the Stanley Cup was in the 1950s.

Our family participated in the parade along with the hockey players and coaches, and we started off the day with a wonderful breakfast with the team at Risata Restaurant at The Second City-Detroit. The team arrived via bus with their wives and children, and the parade organizers assigned everyone a number that corresponded to the float or car they rode in for the parade. Each of the Red Wings players drove in a beautiful, bright red Mustang.

The event began around 11:30 a.m. right in front of the Fox Theatre, and there were people as far as you could see. It was indescribable to see the throng of fans that were there downtown — one million people came down to view the parade. They lined all of Woodward Avenue and filled Hart Plaza. They were sitting on rooftops, windowsills and on ladders, and they were 25 to 30 feet deep. People even were in their boats on the water in the Detroit River to celebrate the event.

We started very slowly down Woodward heading toward Hart Plaza. I was on one of the last floats with all of the children and grandchildren in our family. I loved being at the end because you could see everything happening in front of us. The Parade Company built a breathtaking float which was red and white with the big purple octopus. It featured music, and we danced the entire time while we were giving the Number One sign and partying with everyone on the parade route. My parents were in the car in front of us, and Steve Yzerman and his family were in the car in front of them. I'll never forget the visual of Steve and his wife, Lisa, and their first baby in the parade. Stevie held the Cup up, and I marveled at how long he could hold it, because it weighs about 35 pounds (although it feels like it's 70 pounds when it's over your head). He held it almost the whole time going down the parade route, which took a good two hours. And as the Yzermans moved down Woodward, people just enveloped them. After a while I couldn't see my parents — I had a little anxiety at first, but people were so peaceful and calm and happy, and they just wanted to walk with them and Stevie along the parade route. It was incredible to see one million people come together to celebrate in a happy and peaceful manner, and it was an inspirational day for the Detroit Red Wings, the fans and the city of Detroit.

During the parade that first year the Wings won the Cup, we also did "the pump," where you pump your arms, palms up, as if you're holding the Stanley Cup. As we went down the parade route, we did the pump every few minutes and the fans did, too. It was an action unique to Detroit and was a real Detroit communication — you knew you were in Hockeytown when you did the pump! There are many great hockey towns — Montreal, Toronto and all these great hockey places — but the pump was a very cool way Detroit hockey fans communicated with each other.

When we finally reached Hart Plaza, there were speeches from all of the team members. That also was the year that Vladdy walked across the stage, which was very memorable and wonderful. The fire department did a water show on the river, and it was beautiful to see the boats out on the Detroit River honking their horns.

I have two children, and experiencing this with them and seeing children along the parade route was really, really touching. That was an experience I think they'll remember their whole lives, because who knows when it will be back. Hopefully soon, but who knows?

The Stanley Cup Victory Parade was just an amazing sight, an amazing experience. It was the one time in our community where every walk of life, every person imaginable — children, adults, all types of people — joined together to celebrate the Detroit Red Wings winning the Stanley Cup. The event was just incredible and I'll never forget it. And I can still feel the excitement of that day.

"

It was incredible to see one million people

come together to celebrate in a happy and peaceful manner,

and it was an inspirational day for the Detroit Red Wings,

the fans and the city of Detroit.

"

William Clay Ford Jr. is the chairman of Ford Motor Company
and vice chairman of the Detroit Lions.
Photographed at Greenfield Village in Dearborn,
in the garage where his grandfather made his first car.

From the time I was born in 1957, the holiday season in Detroit has been one of my strongest, most enduring memories of the city. It started every year with Thanksgiving. My whole family would go to the Thanksgiving Day parade and then head over to Tiger Stadium to see the Lions play. It seemed always to snow on Thanksgiving, but it made for a great day.

My father would drive us in his Lincoln Town Car. It was always so cold that my mother would wrap me in about five blankets to watch the game. I thought it was a great time, mostly because she brought an enormous thermos of hot chocolate. I would polish the whole thermos off by half-time. The game to me was incidental — it was just so great to be sitting there drinking hot chocolate in a snowstorm. Actually, in those days, the Lions always gave a very good account of themselves on Thanksgiving. They still do, of course.

There was one game I remember in particular against the Green Bay Packers in the early '60s. The Lions beat a very heavily favored Packers team, and Bart Starr, their quarterback, was mauled by our defensive line. The entire stadium was cheering like crazy. It was an incredibly exciting time. Of all the games we saw, that image will always last for me.

Christmas is my other big memory of growing up in Detroit. We'd go to Hudson's every year. Hudson's downtown during the holidays was an amazing place. The first thing we'd do was see Santa Claus, and after that we'd go to something called the "For Children Only Shop." I think only children under 12 were allowed in there. It gave kids the opportunity to do their own Christmas shopping and, as a kid, I loved it. Our parents would put a couple of dollars in an envelope, and we would go in to shop. I thought I was so grown up because I was actually shopping, without supervision, handling money. My sisters and I would do all our Christmas shopping there. It was a great feeling, and a neat idea.

I don't think I've missed a Thanksgiving Day Lions game since the day I was born; but, since they've been in Auburn Hills, we haven't been able to attend the parade. I can't wait 'til the day we can do both again. When we move the Lions downtown, we will. I think it will be wonderful for my children to have the same Detroit experience that I had growing up — the parade, the football game. Who knows, maybe I'll even take a big thermos of hot chocolate.

Stan Ovshinsky is an inventor and founder of Energy Conversion Devices.
Photographed at ECD Headquarters in Troy.

STAN OVSHINSKY

I was born in Akron, Ohio when it was the rubber capital of the world, and therefore started in the automotive industry at its very base, where the rubber hits the road.

I was very much interested in everything — science, technology, history, art and literature, politics, poetry and girls. I was not interested in school but was very excited by learning and found that I could do it much better on my own.

As a kid, I wanted to be an inventor and a boxer simultaneously. When I was about 11, my father, who had started working at the age of 10, asked me what trade I was going to learn and I said that I wanted to be a toolmaker, which I became. When just out of my teens I invented a new type of machine tool that I called the Benjamin (after my father) Automatic Center Drive. I was able to employ new ideas that I had developed in metal cutting physics and automatic machine control. These machines became quite successful and my work took me to Detroit in the mid 1940s. To me, Detroit was a dream city. It had all the things that interested me — industry, culture, a chance to express my creative ability.

Moving to Detroit permanently at the beginning of 1951, I became a Director of R&D for the Hupp Corporation and invented electric power steering that according to the experts had much superior properties to the hydraulic power steering that was coming into prominent use. Saginaw Steering, a division of General Motors, loved it, but the president of Hupp refused to make the deal.

I pursued my interests in science and invention in parallel, the former through work in neurophysiology where I was invited by Dr. Ernie Gardner, Chairman of the Department of Anatomy and later Dean of Wayne University Medical School, to do collaborative research on my concepts. 1955 was our *annus mirabilis* (miraculous year). Iris and I fell in love and we literally created the field of amorphous and disordered materials. Utilizing these ideas, I made a nerve cell model device that had switching and memory functions and also that could be adaptive and therefore the basis of a learning/intelligent computer.

On January 1, 1960, Iris and I founded Energy Conversion in Detroit in a storefront on McNichols near Schaefer with the express purpose of solving societal problems rather than creating them. We chose energy and information because we felt that the changes needed in these areas would become the basis of the new world economy, the former helping to solve the problems of pollution, climate change and the dangers of war over oil and the latter because new types of information systems would be necessary to make computers truly intelligent with tremendous amounts of memory. We invented new thin-film photovoltaics to convert sunlight into electricity and new rechargeable batteries utilizing hydrogen in the solid form to store energy. We used these same principles to permit hydrogen stored in a solid to be used as a fuel. Hydrogen is considered the ultimate fuel because it is completely non-polluting. We recently formed a strategic alliance with Texaco, a very progressive and forward-thinking oil company that intends to become an energy company through the use of our technology. We are setting up several important joint ventures with them.

Just as our work became the enabling technology in energy, in the information field our optical phase change memories have become the enabling technology for rewritable CD-ROMs and DVDs. In this area we have a strategic alliance with General Electric.

When I invented the Ovonic threshold and memory switches, a common turndown by the scientific and commercial institutions was: "Well, Mr. Ovshinsky, they are digital devices — who in the world would want digital devices? Everyone knows that analog switches have all the answers." Needless to say, the world has gone digital and now we have a joint venture with Intel, the leading semiconductor company.

Our work is very exciting. I invented not only the materials and the products but also the technology to manufacture them. I also originated the scientific base for our work as there was no meaningful activity in our area, since the field of solid state physics was going in the completely opposite direction using crystalline materials. All of our products are called Ovonic, an eponymous term which can be found in dictionaries all over the world.

I was very fortunate through the years to gain the support of many of the leading scientists who represented the heroic age of physics and chemistry — I.I. Rabi, Linus Pauling, Robert Wilson, Sir Nevill Mott, Kenichi Fukui, William Lipscomb and others. I worked in close collaboration with great scientists — Helmut Fritzsche, University of Chicago, David Adler of MIT and many others. I am particularly proud of the splendid team of colleagues and collaborators who work with us at ECD whose contributions are so important in our work.

A major reason that we have enjoyed Detroit has been the many talented people with whom we have worked, including directors of our company. In the last seven years we have been very fortunate to have as our partner Bob Stempel who is the chairman of our company. He is not only truly a giant in the automotive industry, he is also building with us the great new industries needed for our changing world.

We have always been interested in showing the joy and excitement of science to young people and through our Ovonic nickel metal hydride batteries which are the batteries of choice to make electric, hybrid and fuel cell vehicles practical, we have put the romance back into the automotive industry which had drawn me to Detroit in the first place. We have for many years worked with hydrogen, not only for batteries but also as the ultimate clean and plentiful fuel. We want to make Detroit not only the automotive center of the past but of the future.

People have asked why we did not move to Silicon Valley where scientific and technological contributions and entrepreneurship would be much more appreciated and certainly easier to accomplish than in Detroit. Our answer is that we live here and love it and if one wants to change the world using science and technology to solve societal problems, one has to go into the lion's den and struggle there; not in the Ferrari land of instant millionaires, but in the land where cars are built and the problems need solving. The struggle has been well worth it since both the auto companies and the oil companies that were in opposition to us have now joined us.

The new millennium will reflect the hard work that we have put in to change the world for the better. I am very pleased that *Time Magazine* named me a Hero for the Planet, someone who is trying to heal the earth. My childhood vision of a better world has continued to be my driving force. Our five wonderful children and my love of Iris have been my sustenance and inspiration.

"

As a kid, I wanted to be an inventor and a boxer simultaneously.

When I was about 11, my father, who had started working at the age of 10,

asked me what trade I was going to learn and I said that

I wanted to be a toolmaker, which I became.

"

Lily Tomlin is an actress.

Photographed at the home of a friend in Los Angeles, California.

I was originally going to be a doctor. I was in pre-med school at Wayne State. But one day, one of my classmates was leaving after class to read for a play being given at the Bonstelle, *The Madwoman of Chaillot*. On the way out, she said to me — pretty arrogantly — "You should come along, there are a lot of small parts."

So I went over, and of course I was so nervous — I didn't know how to audition for something. But I filled out a piece of paper, and sure enough, they did need a lot of people, they did need a lot of raw extras. So I wound up getting a walk-on; I became one of the Capitalist Women, the mistresses and the wives of the bankers and the industrialists who, according to the sensibilities of the play, were destroying the civilization.

There were three of us who were the Capitalist Women, and we had to go down this big, curving stairway. I would ad lib every time at rehearsal, and all these kids, who were drama majors, thought it was kind of funny, because I would just improvise something comical, and I thought, *Gee, it would be great if I could earn a living doing this.* Because I really enjoyed it, it was great fun. So I went over to the David Mackenzie Hall, which was the men's fraternal union at Wayne State; they had a scholarship fund-raiser thing they did every year, and got a part in that. It was more of a variety show. That's when I first started doing characters. The first character I did was a takeoff on a Grosse Pointe matron.

My mom's maiden name is Ford, so vicariously she loved to read about the Fords in the old society pages of *The Detroit News* and *Detroit Free Press*. Charlotte Ford was making her debut around that time, and they were talking about it in the newspaper. It was months in preparation, it cost

$250,000 at that time, which was a fortune, and they said if you drive around the estate, in the separation between the hedges you could see preparations for the party. My mother wanted to go so badly, so I borrowed a car from a friend; he still lives in Detroit. And it was an old car; one of the doors was tied on with a rope. I said, "Mother, if the car breaks down, it's really going to be embarrassing. We're not going to have any way to get home; we'll have to have someone tow us away." Anyway, we made it, a load of cars were all circling the estate, and sure enough, we looked in and we could see the twinkling lights and things like that as they set up all the stuff.

Years later, I was with one of my friends from Cass Tech High School — her name was Kathy King, who later married Henry Ford II. She and I had been cheerleaders together at Cass Tech. When I played the Fisher in 1989, with *The Search for Signs of Intelligent Life in the Universe*, about 10 or 12 of us girls who had been cheerleaders and hung out at Cass Tech, all got together — not at that Ford Estate, but the estate that she lived in with Henry Ford. And we called my mom on the phone and said, "You can come in the front door now, Mrs. Tomlin."

Ernie Harwell is a baseball announcer.
Photographed at Tiger Stadium in Detroit.

It was 1959 and I was announcing games in Baltimore. I was having a good time — it was my sixth year there, and I was very happy. Then, on the last day of the season in 1959, the Orioles were playing in New York and I got a call from George Kell, who was announcing for the Tigers. He said, "The Tigers are going to make an announcing change, and Mr. Harry Sisson, the Vice President, has asked me if I would call you and find out if you would be interested in coming to Detroit."

George Kell had played for the Orioles. In his waning years, he got hit in the head a couple times. So he had come up to the press box and the radio booth and got some free food, ice cream, Coke and stuff like that, and he found out how nice it was. Once when we were up there I told him, "Why don't you go on — we'll put you on the broadcast and let you call an inning or so." So I put him on, and he sort of liked it. Later, when he quit playing, he got a job in radio with the Tigers. So his calling me for the Tigers' announcing job was sort of a payback, I guess.

When George contacted me, I said, "Well, George, I really like the job I've got, and we're doing fine, but I don't want to close the door on anything."

"Well, why don't you call Mr. Sisson," he said. So I did, and Sisson said to come on out.

In those days, Detroit was far ahead of Baltimore as a baseball town. The Orioles had come into the big leagues in 1954 — they had been the St. Louis Browns, which was a poor franchise; they had moved the team from St. Louis to Baltimore. They were in the development stage and didn't have many good players. The interest in Baltimore wasn't as keen as it was in Detroit, and Baltimore was struggling in attendance; they weren't drawing a million people every year. Meanwhile, Detroit had a long-time established franchise and had the reputation at that time of being the best baseball city in the country. So from the standpoint of baseball, Detroit was a lot better spot for me at that time. Of course, I'd visited Detroit when I was with the Orioles. The first game they ever played in their history was with Detroit in 1954. So I knew about Detroit — we used to stay at the Book Cadillac, which was a nice hotel, and I thought it was a very classy town.

The Briggs family had owned the ball club for a long time. The Briggs sold to a syndicate, and John Fetzer, who was a member of the syndicate, bought it out. And when he bought it out, he decided that they would do away with the Briggs name and just give it the generic name Tiger Stadium. It started out as Bennett Park, then Navin Field, then Briggs Stadium and then Tiger Stadium. So we know a guy's age by what he calls the ballpark. If he says Bennett Park, you know he's old. (Now it will be Comerica Park, so we have a new name to get used to!)

So I flew out during the World Series of '59. They had a chauffeur there at Briggs Stadium who came out and picked me up at the airport and brought me to the ballpark. It seems to me in those days Metro Airport didn't exist; we flew into Willow Run, which made it a lot longer trip — it added another 20 minutes to the trip downtown.

I went to Briggs Stadium and talked to Mr. Sisson, who was sort of a financial man with the Tigers. Very straightforward, very open and, as it turned out, a good guy to work for, very honest. We sat there in his office on the third floor of the building and had a nice interview. "Well," he said, "You know it looks like things are going pretty good, but Stroh Brewery has just bought the broadcast of the games on radio and TV; they're going to sponsor the game completely. So they want you to come over and meet Mr. John Stroh, who's the big boss of Stroh." So I went to the Stroh Brewery, met Mr. Stroh, he was a very down-to-earth, pleasant kind of a guy, and we got along well. They took me through the brewery, we had lunch over there, and I met all the Stroh people.

Then, to consummate the deal, we went back to Tiger Stadium. They made me an offer, the people back in Baltimore couldn't meet it, so I decided to come. It was pretty much a business proposition.

I had gotten married in '41, so I'd been married 18 years at that time. And Lulu loved her old home in Baltimore. We had an old farmhouse right in town, a beautiful old place built in 1850 that had eight bedrooms and eight baths and two acres of land. She didn't want to leave, but she was a good sport and she pulled up stakes and came along with me.

So we came on. I figured they've got a good franchise, a high-class operation, it's always been a great baseball town. I reported to the Tigers for work in March of 1960.

I'm sort of a Johnny-come-lately; I haven't been around here as long as some folks. But I have seen a lot of Tigers history in my years here. And baseball history in general has always been important to me. We had a collection of 90,000 clippings sorted and indexed (some from back in the 1880s) ... books on baseball ... baseball pictures ... we had about four or five rooms in the basement filled in Grosse Pointe. We gave it to the Detroit Public Library, so now people go down and use that collection. We have a little bit of Tiger history on our front porch, too. About 15 years ago I got a couple of old stadium seats from Briggs Stadium or maybe Navin Field. They've got a nice little filigree on the side, with a Tiger in cast iron with a bat over his shoulder. Those are the really good ones. We had them mounted on a wooden platform, because they're not free standing, and they're out on our front porch. The original color of them was that nice dark forest green, but the color clashed with the exterior of our house, according to my wife. So when I went on a trip, she decided she'd paint them black. But I'm getting even. The black's peeling off now and the original green is coming back. Revenge! The revenge of the peeling paint.

I love the people in Michigan, they've been so receptive and so great to me; they've treated us well. We get away a few months in the winter, we don't like the snow and ice except on Christmas cards, but other than that, it's been really great. Like my song says, *"Michigan and Trumbull ... there's never been a corner like Michigan and Trumbull."*

"

Michigan and Trumbull . . .

there's never been a corner like Michigan and Trumbull.

"

Elmore Leonard is an author.
Photographed at what was The Abington in Detroit.

In the fall of 1934, I arrived in Detroit with a southern accent, a blend of New Orleans, where I was born, Dallas, Oklahoma City and Memphis. I was nine, and for awhile kids kept after me to say things like "honey chile" and "sugah," getting a kick out of the way I spoke. My mother took offense saying, "They should talk — listen to how they roll their R's." My mother believed northern women all had big feet.

My friends and I went to Blessed Sacrament grade school, on Belmont behind the cathedral, and played on Woodward Avenue. Woodward was our street in that period from '35 to '39, the area around Collingwood and Trowbridge. Summer nights we played a game called Hot Ass (sometimes referred to as Hot Cooloo, though no one knew why). One of the kids would hide a leather belt in a vacant lot, a storefront awning, behind a billboard, anywhere. The rest of us would roam around looking for the belt. Then, whoever found it would yell, "Hot ass!" — or, "Hot cooloo!" — and use the belt to swat as many guys as he could before we got back safely to a corner lightpole.

We played football and baseball on "Sweeney's Field," a lot at the corner of Boston Boulevard and John R. Our uniforms were red and black sweatshirts. Girls from our class would lead a cheer that went, "Red and black attack attack! Red and black attack attack! Who attacks? We attack ..." and so on. The team we played most often, the Harmon Street Gang, stole all their equipment from the Sears store in Highland Park.

Saturdays, we caught the matinee at the Fisher, watched Ken Maynard and Tom Mix serials, and ran around the theater if the main attraction was *Camille,* or anything like it.

We lived in the Abington, an apartment-hotel on Seward five blocks north of the GM building, where my dad worked. The Abington dining room offered dinner selections during those Depression years that ranged from 40 to 60 cents an entree. We played in the halls, swiped rolls from room service tables and ran for our lives when Monty the bellman came after us.

Those years, streetcars were rattling up and down Woodward Avenue from the fairgrounds to the river. We'd hop aboard and ride downtown to Hudson's to visit the toy department, or to the Vernor's ginger ale plant, then at the foot of Woodward. You'd get free samples if you took the tour. Sometimes on Sundays we'd board the ferry to Windsor and ride back and forth for a nickel.

The streetcar fare, 70 cents, was good for a transfer if you wanted to change at Clairmount or go out East Jefferson. I rode the Jefferson car to the Altes lager brewery — "The Beer in the Green Bottle" — where I worked after finishing at U of D High and before going into the Navy. There was a reefer you could walk in and grab a cold one any time you were thirsty. I worked at Altes not much more than a week before my mother made me quit, wanting to know if I was coming home happy from work or a party.

Detroit has changed a lot since then. They've added freeways and sold the streetcars to Mexico City, and all the new buildings seem to be in Southfield and Troy. But whenever I'm away and someone asks where I live, I always say Detroit. It's still my hometown.

Jim Brandstatter is a sports producer and commentator. Robbie Timmons is a television news anchor.

Photographed at St. Mary's Church, Greektown, in Detroit.

The truth is, there isn't enough room. To begin is a mistake, because you can't finish. No matter where you go in the story, there is more to relate. More to remember.

As a little boy growing up in East Lansing, Detroit was always a special place to go. Grandma Brandstatter lived on Jefferson in Ecorse. My dad, a former Detroit cop, piled the five boys in the Chevy wagon, and off we went, thrilled with anticipation to see Grandma. She would fix piles of chicken paprikash and other Hungarian delights. We gorged ourselves. Then it was off to Briggs Stadium to see the annual Detroit Police Field Day. The tug of war was my favorite. The smell of the stadium was my next favorite. Detroit was a special place even at home. When Dad would watch the Lions play on our grainy black-and-white TV, I could sense the importance of the team to him. "See number 22, that's Bobby Layne," my dad would say with reverence. *Layne must be special,* I thought; *he played for Detroit.*

Detroit had to be special because some days my mom would get all dressed up and leave home with her friends before I left for school. "Where you going, Mom?" I would ask. "Your mother and her friends are going to Detroit. We are going shopping at Hudson's," she would say with a smile. *Wow,* I thought.

Detroit was special because I got to see Gordie Howe play at the Olympia on Safety Patrol Day. It was the Red Wings against Montreal. Mr. Howe uncorked an elbow on John Ferguson and I knew why Mr. Howe was special.

Detroit was special when I got my driver's license. Mom and Dad let me go to Detroit for a double-header against the Yankees. My buddies and I took binoculars. We trained them on Mickey Mantle. We sat in Kaline's corner. We ate the best hot dogs in the world. It smelled the same. It was special.

When we left the game, we laughed, excited about the day. We passed state police cars speeding downtown as we headed home on the Lodge. About the time we got to Brighton the radio told us why the state police were in such a hurry. Detroit was burning. The riots of '67 had started.

Detroit became special again in '68. The Tigers won a World Series, healing the wounds of the previous summer. I was on the practice field in Ann Arbor as a freshman football player at Michigan when Bill Freehan squeezed the final out. Practice stopped; it was special.

Detroit was special because I worked on an assembly line. I put torque converters in transmissions in Livonia. I straightened steel in Hamtramck. It was working Detroit. The men and women who do it for a lifetime are special people. They are the backbone of a great city. They are Detroiters, and they are special.

When I started in broadcasting, I always wanted to work in Detroit. It was a major market. I made it in 1977, working for WDIV-TV Channel 4.

Robbie had come to Detroit in '76 as a "big time" anchor of the 6 and 11 p.m. news on WJBK-TV2. We had met in Jackson the year before, and we were dating. Together, we discovered more of Detroit. The Ren Cen had just finished construction of its top floors, and we felt a sense of rebirth. The towering cylinders were signaling the beginning of the renaissance of Detroit, and both Robbie and I felt we were in on the ground floor.

We both worked the late shift, so after work we'd meet downtown. The Lindell AC was our jumping-off point. Jimmy and Johnny Butsicaris took us to Greektown. Lamb chops at 2 a.m. at the Grecian Gardens was special. Yelling good night to Sam the Cabbie was a moment I looked forward to on many nights. He would yell "Good night family, wherever you are," and duck out the back door with a six-pack in a brown paper bag. We would holler back, "Good night, Sam!" He was "Norm" of the TV series *Cheers* before Norm ever existed.

The Lindell provided us with entertainment, food, a place to laugh and a place to cry. We met and forged friendships with the likes of Woody Herrman; Sonny Eliot and his lovely wife, Annette; Andre the Giant; countless coaches and athletes; and a fair number of broadcasters in the hallowed halls on the corner of Cass and Michigan. It was, and still is, a special place.

Singing Irish songs at the Tipperary Pub with Tom O'Halloran was special. The Roostertail during the Gold Cup races was special. Getting lost at the Ren Cen was special. Dinner at the Press Club was special. Carl's Chop House, Little Harry's, The Whitney, Jim's Garage, the Caucus Club, the London Chop House, the Anchor Bar — they were all special. They were the part of Detroit Robbie and I discovered together, and that was truly special.

In 1980, we decided to get married. I was hosting a Tigers pre-game show that summer and on a Saturday night I went to Mass in Greektown. I knew that night where we would get married.

Our rehearsal dinner was at the Old Parthenon in Greektown with Tommy Peristeris as our host. The next day we were married at St. Mary's Church in Greektown. It was special. It was Detroit.

In 1982, I was given the opportunity to be a part of a pair of Detroit's storied traditions — WXYZ-TV Channel 7, and her co-anchor was the legendary Bill Bonds. This privilege continues today and into the next millennium.

Meanwhile, I have been lucky enough to work for the likes of WJR, WWJ and WXYT. All of them are broadcast giants, and the great electronic voices of the Midwest. For both of us, the city has been the backdrop of special careers.

We have been fortunate to experience the flavors of the city, and share with Detroiters the enthusiasm over its bright future.

We've been fortunate to be able to tell the world, through our broadcasting jobs, that Detroit people are generous, kind and eager to help each other. They also exhibit a tremendous pride in their city and a dogged determination to keep making it better. Detroiters are like the city they love: resilient, tough, hardworking, faithful and proud.

This is a special time for Detroit. We're fortunate to be witnesses to its new vitality.

Our memories of Detroit, the way it was, will always be special, and our involvement in its future is a special gift.

"

'See number 22, that's Bobby Layne,'

my dad would say with reverence.

Layne must be special, I thought;

he played for Detroit.

"

Jeff Daniels is an actor.
Photographed at Tiger Stadium in Detroit.

The only gods on earth I ever saw were in Tiger Stadium. Having spent a great deal of time in Hollywood, I know a god when I see one. Personally speaking, I've never considered myself to be anything close to divine, though after several years of being treated as if I were larger than life, I'm certainly not above taking that undeserved piousness and using it to my advantage. One of the perks of living an exalted existence is being able to get into places the unexalted can't. I was an hour early for my appointment with the Tiger-Staff-Person-In-Charge-Of-Dealing-With-Celebrities-Who-Want-To-Get-On-The-Field.

He couldn't have been more polite.

"I've been looking forward to this day my whole life," I told him, with my brand-new Tiger cap sitting on top of my head like a new puppy.

"Follow me," he said with just enough regality.

To step onto the field at the corner of Michigan and Trumbull is to suddenly make sense of everything Thomas Boswell ever wrote. The smell of the grass. The crack of the bat. The face of a boy in every player. On a gorgeous summer night it was raining our national pastime and with over 80 years of Tiger history underneath me I let it drench me to my soul. When he asked if I wanted to sit in the dugout, I almost wept. I entered it as if I were entering Shakespeare's study. Even through the padding, the bench was hard. The wall behind me was coated with years of enamel that failed to hide the

cracks. Decades of spikes had gnawed away at the planks beneath my feet. I sat where they had been, trying to feel all those seasons, all those games, inning after inning, play after play, pitch after pitch. I looked out to second base and saw Gibby rounding the bag, stretching a double into a triple. I looked towards home plate and saw Mickey Cochrane jogging back to the dugout with Schoolboy Rowe, leaving a stunned Ted Williams standing at the plate staring daggers into the umpire. I looked out to the right field corner and saw Number 6 whirl and throw a rope on a line all the way to Wert's glove. I looked over and saw Hal Newhouser and Frank Lary laughing at a young Jack Morris jamming a baseball between his fingers while Rocky Colavito tried to explain the arc of Whitey Ford's curve to Hank Greenberg as George Kell kept telling anybody who'd listen *if you want hot try spending August in Arkansas* and way down at the end of the bench, all by himself, was Cobb, his glare piercing through me as if it had been shot out of a gun.

Higginson hit a batting practice fastball into the upper deck in right. I looked down at the tunnel leading off to the locker room. With the clock ticking on my celebrity status, and banking on the fact that famous people can go anywhere, I slipped out of the dugout and into the darkness.

About halfway up the tunnel was a urinal. No door, no stall, just this archaic trough stuck against the wall. The porcelain was stained with rust. The pipes were leaking. Water was running endlessly. I stood there thinking of all those players. All those teams. All those seasons. I turned back towards the light coming in from the field, spilling onto the floor of the tunnel. *Ty Cobb peed here. Al Kaline peed here. Mickey Cochrane peed here …*

Bill Frieder is a retired college basketball coach.

Photographed in Ann Arbor.

Mornings came early for me as a kid. My father owned a produce company in Saginaw, Michigan called Florida Market. Every Monday and Thursday we would drive to Detroit, and we'd leave at one or two in the morning to get to Eastern Market or the Terminal. You had to be there early — you needed to get there at four or five in the morning so you could make your purchases and get what you needed early. And you always wanted to get out of there by noon so you could get back, unload it all and get ready for the rest of the week. We'd always shoot to be out of there by noon.

We drove a big semi with a trailer. I'd ride with my dad or my grandfather when I was very young in the late '40s, and then when I was 16 years old, I sometimes drove the truck to Detroit and did it by myself.

Everybody's heard of or been to Eastern Market, but not many people knew about the Terminal, which I believe used to be over on Fort Street. I don't know if it's still there. We went to the Terminal more in the winter. Railroad cars would come in from all over the country; it was just a huge bunch of buildings where people had different stalls, and people would buy train carloads — carloads of watermelons,

carloads of onions, carloads of potatoes. The Terminal serviced a lot of people; they'd come from all over Michigan and northern Ohio. I remember buying from a place there called Schwartz and Company, and Larry Horowitz was a big seller back then, too. We did more business at Eastern Market in the summer, because the farmers there sold more home-grown produce like tomatoes, lettuce and stuff like that.

Whether you went to Eastern Market or the Terminal, it was all about supply and demand. And a lot of bargaining. If you needed strawberries and there were a lot of them, you could bargain for a real good price. On the other hand, if something was scarce you could tell as soon as you got there you'd have to pay a high dollar.

What we bought would depend upon the time of the year. All year long we would have to have everything that makes up salad, like lettuce, tomato, cucumber, carrots, green peppers and those things. We'd also have to have all the fruit; lemons, grapefruit, oranges, limes, etc. Then, depending on the time of year, we'd also get things like potatoes and onions.

You'd have to buy what you needed, fill your truck, load it up, and by noon you'd head back. When we got back to Saginaw we'd inventory it and get it sold on Tuesday and Wednesday, then go back on Thursday. It was a lot of driving. But as much as we made that long trip, we never seemed to get tired of Detroit. My dad would take me to Tiger games on the weekends; I think that's what got me interested in sports. When my wife, Jan, and I first started dating, we'd drive down to catch Tiger games on the weekends or go to Kensington. And also, obviously getting a bachelor's degree and a master's degree from the University of Michigan, and later coaching at U. of M. for 17 years, led to many trips from Ann Arbor to Detroit for ball games, social events and other matters. So the drive to Detroit has always been a part of my life.

Our business was on 1620 Bagley Street in Saginaw. It was in business from 1931 to 1986, when my dad passed away. We serviced the foundry, the steering gear plant and the Chevrolet and Buick plants, and we'd also service the restaurants in Frankenmuth like Zehnders and Bavarian Inn, delivering their potatoes and cabbage and cucumbers — all the stuff that they serve with their chicken — plus we serviced other stores, restaurants and cafeterias. When I went back there recently, I went by the building and took pictures; the sign's still up at the building.

And the signs of that time are still in my life today. Working in the family business had a tremendous impact on my character, characteristics and my personality. It equipped me to handle long, hard hours and taught me responsibility, work ethics and attention to detail. All the things that matter in coaching, really. You had to sell produce or throw it away. You have to recruit ball players or lose games. It was my family business that led me to what I am today.

"

You had to sell produce or throw it away.

You have to recruit ball players or lose games.

It was my family business that led me to what I am today.

"

Maurice Lezell is the founder of Belvedere Construction.
Photographed at his home in Birmingham.

Some of the best things in life come to you, not by trying to accomplish them specifically, but just by being natural, by being yourself.

I've been in the remodeling business for over 50 years. The business just came to me back in the '40s — a long time ago — just because I happened to be there and willing to work. I started with storm windows. They didn't have replacement windows at that time; storm windows were the big thing. Then one thing led to another. I started doing siding and at one time even built homes, but I wasn't happy doing that. The business just accumulated. Never wanting to take profit and run away with it, I always doubled up and tripled up and did things to make it bigger and bigger. It's gotten to be a real big business now.

It really is a crazy thing. I never started Belvedere Construction with the idea of becoming "Mr. Belvedere," never started with the idea of going further with it. And when it did take off, I became a part of it. In other words, it was never deliberately planned. It just happened. Even the Belvedere name just happened. There was a street called Belvedere that I enjoyed in Detroit, there was a movie, *Mr. Belvedere Goes To College,* at that time, and I just thought it would sound nice as a name.

And I wasn't the first business owner to be on TV. Other people in the car business or furniture business were there long before me. But I was the first one to realize the power and potential and capitalize on it. In doing segments on the air with Bill Kennedy and Conrad Patrick, being involved with promoting charities, people got to know the name Belvedere, and we just kept getting bigger. We became very involved with the State Fair when their attendance was low. Our motto was "Save The State Fair. Go There." We had all kinds of celebrities talking about the State Fair, and we hope it made an impact on people's consciousness of the fair. We had Mr. Belvedere Clubs; we had a look-alike contest that was so successful it was on the front page of *The Detroit News.* All kinds of other things went on, most of which had nothing to do with remodeling.

From 1970 to 1980, I was doing short remodeling TV segments — interviews on the air with Bill Kennedy and Conrad Patrick. I'd get done with Channel 50 and then run over to Channel 9. We were going crazy with TV. Our advertising budget was overwhelming — we were one of the biggest local advertisers in Detroit at that time.

Of course, Bill Kennedy is gone now. He and I had a good rapport. Bill was one of the best interrogators in the whole business, in Detroit. He was good. He really drew out the people. He knew what he was doing; he was a good actor. But it's amazing, just amazing how many people I meet today who tell me, "I grew up with you. I was watching you on Bill Kennedy when I was four years old. I watched you when I came home from school." Look at all the seeds we planted without even knowing it! We did the shows with the idea of getting the old people to call us with some leads, not with the idea of reaching kids. It's amazing how many seeds we planted.

Conrad Patrick was on Channel 9. At that time, Channel 9 in Canada was beamed to Detroit, and they had Detroit advertising. Conrad and I made tapes in Windsor — two-minute tapes, which is almost an impossibility today. They were tremendous sellers, great for results. We used to make them extemporaneously; we didn't have anything typed. So one day, Conrad said to me, in the very hard way, as he always would, "Why would I call you before I called anybody else? Why would I want you to do my work for me?" Without thinking, I said, "Conrad, we do good work."

And it stuck.

Our biggest theme before that was "Have No Fear With Belvedere." But after that we threw everything out and started with "We Do Good Work."

Again, these things weren't done with the idea of creating a slogan or an image; we did them with the idea of being natural. Soretta Mozier, an advertising consultant who worked with us for 10 years used to say, "I wish I could have a TV camera right at your desk and just tape you for a whole day. I'd probably have enough script to last an entire year."

I'm never satisfied. I've always felt that I could go further. I had this big business going, and about 15 years ago I decided to go to acting school in New York. I spent four days in New York and three days in Detroit going back and forth. It got to be too much. The only thing acting school taught me was that I'm not an actor. I was very happy that they told me I wasn't worth much, so I could go back and do what I was doing. But I can make tapes. I'm good for 30 seconds and that's about it. In a play or anything like that,

I just don't like having to memorize, and I found I just wasn't good at it. When you watch a play or a movie, can you imagine the amount of memorization they must go through to get to that stage? That's a hard job!

It was too rushed for me. It's pretty hard to run a business in Detroit, then go to acting school in New York and memorize your lines; it was a difficult situation. You either have to go to school and stay there and learn, or don't go. I tried to compromise, I just felt I could overcome anything at that earlier age. I guess if they had told me how good I was, and that I should be there, and be an actor, then that would have been something else. But no one ever gave me any compliments. I really didn't give it a good strong try, either. So here I am.

I'm almost retired, and I still have a desire to go to New York or LA and just for the fun of it go through it again — I'd have more time to devote to acting.

But until then, I am enjoying working here. People have grown to trust us. That all started from advertising. My greatest pleasure now is when I come to work, two or three old customers call with referrals. Someone will call and say we did a job for her mother, and now she wants a job done for herself. This is something that makes me feel good, because somewhere along the line we did something right. I'm not going to say that we make them all happy. Because in this business, when you do the amount of volume we do, you're going to get people who aren't. But when people are happy, that's where I get my satisfaction. You build on that. You build and you build. You plant seeds.

"

Without thinking, I said,

"Conrad, we do good work."

And it stuck.

"

Joe Schmidt is a retired NFL player and coach.
Photographed at Detroit Country Day High School in Beverly Hills.

I arrived here with very little fanfare.

I was drafted by the Lions in 1953. First of all, I didn't want to come here. I actually wanted to be drafted by Pittsburgh. The Steelers had been interested in me, so I had it all planned out — I was going to get through school and play for the Pittsburgh Steelers. They had said they were going to draft me in the first, second or third round. It never happened. (The reason they gave me was because my senior year I had some extensive injuries and missed maybe three games. They thought I was injured and didn't want to waste a draft choice on me.) So I was very disappointed when I got drafted by Detroit in the 7th round.

When I got here, I reported to training camp, which was at Eastern Michigan. At the time it was called Michigan State Normal College; it was a very small school at that time. (And of course, we played our games at Tiger Stadium, which was called Briggs Stadium then.)

At training camp, they assigned us numbers. The equipment man asked me, "What number do you want?" I said, "I don't care," so he threw me jersey 64.

It was "Picture Day" at training camp; it's actually like a PR day — the press and everybody comes out. Naturally that was a big day for the Lions, being that they had just won a championship the year before. They had everybody out on the field, and they took everybody's picture. I was the last one there, and no one said anything to me. They didn't call my name or anything. They didn't even take my picture. I figured, "Oh boy, I'm in big trouble; they don't even know I'm here."

I came here with not too much hope of making the team, because the Lions had won the championship. Generally when teams win a championship, they don't change the players too much. But as it turned out, I was pleasantly surprised. I had an opportunity to play, and during that particular pre-season game I won a job. The rest fell into place after that and I've been here ever since.

Before I was born, my mom, dad and my oldest brother, John, had lived in Detroit for a short time. My dad came up from Pittsburgh because they were paying $5 a day at Ford Motor Company. That was supposed to be big money back then. They lived in a downstairs flat in Delray, and they became good friends with the woman who lived upstairs, who was from Hungary. In that area at that time there were a lot of Hungarian people. My mother and father were both immigrants — my father was part German and part Hungarian, and my mother was German descent. I think they hit it off with the woman upstairs because of the fact that they were all new to this country. They stayed in Detroit for a while until my mother got homesick. That was the first time she'd ever been away from Pittsburgh, so eventually she demanded they move back there.

About midway through the Lions' 1953 season, my mom and John drove up from Pittsburgh to visit me. My mother asked me to drive by that old place where they lived. She had a hard time locating it, but finally we found it. I said, "Maybe the woman still lives there. For the heck of it, let's just knock on the door." So we did, and she answered! She was very surprised — it was quite a shock after all those years, suddenly your neighbor reappears under different circumstances. But we had a nice reunion.

We had a great group of guys on the Lions team that year — we meshed very well from the standpoint of physical attributes and mental attributes. In the evenings we used to hang at a place called Kelly's, a bar-restaurant down on Waterman and Dix. After the ball games we would go down to Kelly's and drink a little beer and celebrate or commiserate whatever happened that day. The Kellys were wonderful people; they had four sons that we hung around with. Mr. and Mrs. Kelly always took care of the ballplayers. Mrs. Kelly was sort of a mother hen — she'd spoil the heck out of us, waiting for us to show up, making sure we were fed, making sure everything was fine. Most of the guys on the team were married, so their wives would come down, we'd sit in the back room off by ourselves, it was a sort of private area. That's where we ended up the night we won the championship in 1953. There wasn't any big fanfare like there is today, you've got the Superbowl, and a lot of TV coverage. There was TV coverage back then, but a long way from what it is today. These players today are almost like movie stars; everybody knows them. Back then, people in town knew who we were, but on a national level, unless they were real football fans, you could walk around anyplace and nobody would know who you were. And the money was certainly not what it is today. We made a pittance compared to what players make now. But everything in life is like that.

Playing for the Detroit Lions turned out to be a dream come true for me. As a youngster, playing football was my ambition — my older brothers played football. John had played in college and two years for the Pittsburgh Steelers, so I wanted to play in college, too, and after college I wanted to play professionally. It was a youngster's dream come true — and then to play in the championship as a rookie in 1953 was even more than I ever anticipated. It was just a great experience. It's hard to describe the feeling I had, what it was like being placed in this atmosphere and environment. I loved doing the things I wanted to do as a youngster, and I loved being here at the time when football was just starting as far as television was concerned, and being a part of its development. It's been a wonderful experience here.

"

I had it all planned out

— I was going to get through school and play for the Pittsburgh Steelers.

They had said they were going to draft me in the first,

second or third round. It never happened.

"

Jennifer Granholm is Michigan Attorney General.
Photographed at the Damon J. Keith Elementary School in Detroit.

I married Michigan. My husband and I met in law school at Harvard. He comes from a very large Irish Catholic family in Inkster, so when we married, we moved back here. There was really no question about where we would live; it was the thing to do. The first time I visited it was such a warm experience, and I remember thinking, "These folks from Michigan are really down to earth and welcoming." That's sort of the broad-brush first impression I have of Michigan … the warmth.

And Detroit … well, Detroit is the center of the universe. When we were first married we lived in Indian Village, in the apartments, at the Parkstone — it was a wonderful community. My husband rode his bike down to work on good days. Later, when we lived in Rosedale Park, we'd drive to work taking Grand River instead of going down the freeways, because despite the fact that there were problems on Grand River, and a lot of the buildings had deteriorated, it's our city. We felt that we wanted to see and be a part of the fabric here. Detroit is where all the action is. Of course the folks in the capitol often think *that's* where the action is, and certainly there's a lot of action in Lansing, but to me, Detroit is the place where the center of my life is. I have so many people I love here … friends … colleagues … people who have helped me along the way … people whom I've helped along the way … I just feel like this is the network of my growing up as a lawyer. One person who helped me is Damon Keith, on the Federal Court of Appeals.

I clerked for him as a Federal Judicial Law Clerk — my first job out of law school. I was thrilled to work for him because I had been the editor in chief at Harvard of the *Civil Rights/Civil Liberties Law Review,* and he was one of the heads of the Civil Rights Commission. He's very well known in civil rights circles, so it was a real honor to be selected. He's also an icon in Detroit; he's done so many things as a role model and for people.

He was the first African-American Chief Judge of the Federal District Court here, the first to be appointed to the Sixth Circuit Court of Appeals on the Federal level, last year he was selected the best Federal judge in the nation; he just is a wonderful, wonderful man. Working for him was a good introduction to Detroit as well because he knows everybody in Detroit, and as his law clerk you go to all these events, a great way to be introduced to this marvelous city. I learned to love the city through his eyes.

I was one of three law clerks at the time, and he took us almost everywhere that he went. One of the places he took us that really stands out in my mind is a school that's named after him, the Damon J. Keith Elementary School. I think the occasion was one of the early anniversaries of the school's opening. The kids in the school put on a concert for us in the gym, and it's hard to describe the experience except to say it was off the charts — it was so beautiful that I cried. The songs that were sung and the spirit there of hope and of possibilities … even though it is a public school, the songs contained an element of faith. Because Judge Keith is such a role model for possibilities, they sang to him. It was just a very beautiful moment for a city that had been battered in a lot of ways. It was a small school; there were probably not more than 50 kids in the choir. This group had sung for events before — they were very talented, and their singing had been recognized outside of their school. It was particularly striking that they were only elementary school age — it was marvelous to see kids so young with such talent and spirit. It was just a very uplifting experience. That was very much a highlight.

JENNIFER GRANHOLM

I see that same spirit of hope and possibility in the city today. I think downtown the Campus Martius development and the point from Grand Circus Park down to Jefferson on Woodward that is being looked at, all the energy that's going on there is going to be phenomenal. There's been a lot of job creation and there's been a lot of excitement, people are coming back, GM coming back to the Ren Cen is fantastic, what they plan on doing there is a terrific commitment. And I think it's great that the state has bought the GM building; that's very exciting to me.

There's something about a central downtown of a major city. People try to replicate it outside, but there is only one true downtown. This is the hub of the world.

"

Detroit is the place where the center of my life is.

I have so many people I love here ... friends ... colleagues ...

people who have helped me along the way ... people whom I've helped along the way ...

I just feel like this is the network of my growing up as a lawyer.

"

Pablo Bonilla is a former gang leader who now is married and employed. Photographed at an underpass in southwest Detroit.

I grew up in southwest Detroit at Lafayette and Green. I didn't get to know my dad, just my mom and my two brothers, Luce and Carlos. My mom tried her best with us; she went to school and work. But once we hit high school, I just went away. I was always the quiet type.

I was 15 or 16 when I joined a gang called the Detroit Kings. A few gangs were bothering me and a bunch of other kids, so we started our own, just to retaliate. There were just six of us to start off. We ended up kind of deep, 50 or 60 here, then in Toledo and River Rouge. We expanded to about 170. I was the leader. It was kind of wild, I mean, it seemed like something I wanted to do. I liked it back then; I liked having a lot of power.

A man named Alex Montaner had contacted me. He founded GRACE — Gang Retirement and Continued Education. I blew him off — I didn't want him messing with my set.

I did end up in prison — three months in one place and almost 18 months in a federal prison called Milan. It didn't scare me. I knew I was going, one way or the other. You think you're so strong, then after awhile, it breaks you. You just think, *I did all this, and for what?* They take everything from you. I'm not saying it's bad or good, but it can be good for some people. I don't know where I'd be if I hadn't gotten locked up and had all that time to think.

When I got out, Alex and I kind of got in touch with each other. He completely helped me turn my life around. He sets up this month-and-a-half program like he's a place of business, so we can practice interviewing. At first, when we were all sitting there, members of different gangs, there was a lot of tension. He made us say something friendly to each other, and the tension broke after a couple of hours. We met at a church, so we had to show respect. Pretty soon we were laughing and having fun. Some of us who were there had actually chased

each other down, shot at each other. Now we go out to clubs together. I've met people and they wouldn't even believe we were in a gang before, the way we think and the way we do things. My enemies are now my friends. We work together, hang out together. It stopped a lot of the violence here in Southwest Detroit.

One night last summer — in 1997 — six or seven shots were fired right across the street from where I live. These guys were my enemies, but I went to the guy who was shot. I picked him up and held him, I called the ambulance, held him and talked to him until the police and ambulance came.

Alex's group made it possible for 60 or 70 of us to get employed. My opportunity came from Carmen Munoz, the owner of Munoz Machine. She gave about 20 of us the chance to work without any experience. She figured if we could be dedicated to a gang, we could be dedicated to work, something that benefits us. She just took us in. We're some of her best workers now. I'm production manager and shipping and receiving manager. I'm one of the ones that's really made it. Every day, I get up at six, start at seven. After work I play with my kids for awhile, spend time with my wife. On the weekends, the kids go to their grandma's. The owner of my company is going to try to help me open a business — I'm going to take some classes. They're helping me out a lot.

Being out of gangs took a big load off of me. I don't have to worry about the hassles anymore. I go to schools and churches and outreach centers to help parents teach their kids about staying out of gangs. I'm going to help my brothers, too, and I'm trying to set up jobs for my brothers' friends. Whatever I can do. I took a lot out of the community when I was out there. Now I want to put something back in.

Brenda Goodman is an artist.
Photographed on the roof of her studio in New York City, New York.

Moments frozen. I can taste them. Silver memories melting. Eighteen, a young art student driving to school in my first car, a black 1961 VW. (Not very Detroit, I admit. My next car was a hunter green Mustang convertible, which I had for years.) I lived and breathed art, 24 hours a day, and sometimes fell asleep sitting on a bench, an unfinished painting in front of me, a paint brush still in my hand. A few of us art students hung out together competing with and challenging each other, sitting in a corner taking a break, smoking and drinking coffee with cream and sugar from glass bottles. I felt so full of dreams and hopes. I loved every minute of every day in art school. And then walking down the street to the Detroit Institute of Arts, standing in front of a Rembrandt being totally enraptured by the way he applied paint — how he created life from it. Standing in front of a Van Eyck, a Nolde, a Kokoschka, a Dubuffet, a Guston and, oh yes, the wonderful painting by Degas of his aunt.

And then the years following art school, a group of us known as the Cass Corridor artists, meeting every morning in the courtyard of the D.I.A. — drinking coffee, smoking, reading the *Detroit Free Press.* Some of us talking with each other, some silent, some still with hangovers from the night before. This every-morning ritual filled so many needs—a need to belong, a need for a family of peers and a need for respect. And when we weren't there, we gathered around Ken and Ann Mikolowski's kitchen table. They were Detroit's *Alternative Press* — poems, broadsides, books, original art, done by us for their subscriber packages. We ate, laughed, cried, did art and traded art with eight-year-old Michael, their son, around that table, and had such fine times.

My one-person show in 1973 at the Willis Gallery was like no other that I've ever had. It was my first. So much praise and appreciation of my talents. It was great. I had a good bottle of red wine in one hand and on the other a watch. Looking at the time — not wanting it to end. In two hours it would be over. I wanted it to go on forever. I kept wanting to push back the time. In 1974, John Hallmark Neff came to Detroit as the new curator of contemporary art at the D.I.A. My second show was up at the Gertrude Kasle Gallery in the Fisher Building. He saw it, bought a painting for himself and wanted the museum to purchase one called *"The Cat Approaches."* The day the purchase was approved, I walked over to the D.I.A. to see it. My eyes didn't even see the painting. They were glued to the label next to it.

BRENDA GOODMAN, AMERICAN
BORN 1943–

What a thrill that was. My heart raced. 24 years later, when I think about that day — seeing my name among the great artists in the Detroit Institute's collection still thrills me.

And though I've lived in NYC for the past 22 years, I still go back for shows of my work every couple of years. Sometimes here in NYC, sitting in Soho with a friend, drinking a cappuccino — memories rush in of all those cups of coffee with my friends in art school, in Greektown, at the D.I.A., and in my studio, alone, with a painting I was working on back then.

Ted Nugent is a musician, author, publisher and hunting advocate.

Photographed at "Tedquarters" — Ted Nugent United Sportsman of America headquarters — in Jackson.

I remember one very moving experience that to this day represents probably the threshold of all my musical motivation. It was about 1960; I had a band called the Lourdes in Detroit — we were a force to reckon with in our youth. The band members were Tom Noel on drums, of the famous Noel brothers; Peter Prim on bass; John Finley on rhythm guitar; and John Brake on lead vocals. We're talking a long time ago — I was just a kid, going on 12 that year, mesmerized by all things guitar twang. All the rest of the guys in my band were a few years older than I was.

We were opening up at the Walled Lake Casino, out there near Novi in Walled Lake, for the Billy Lee and the Rivieras band, which eventually became Mitch Ryder and the Detroit Wheels. The Walled Lake Casino burned down in the mid- or late '60s. It looked like it had been built as a skating rink, design-wise, but whenever we were there, it was a dance hall. It was always packed; the girls had their beehive hairdos, and the boys had their stiletto shoes and their pompadours. I was raised in a very disciplined family, and I wasn't allowed to have that kind of hair or those kinds of clothes; I oftentimes felt like a fish out of water, but I could play Chuck Berry licks, so they let me play in the band.

We saw everybody there from Martha and the Vandellas to Gene Pitney to Billy Lee and the Rivieras and the Ides of March, and every rock and roll band that existed back then. It was very electrifying because it was a new era. There was no system in place. PAs were experimental. Guitar amplifiers were experimental. We were in musical cultivation and idea exploratory mode. It was a very moving time, and I'm just so pleased I had been born at the right time to be there.

We were playing there on a weekend (I was so young, I wasn't allowed out except on weekends). I think Lee Allen might have been the MC; he's quite a landmark in our musical history as well — he was the disc jockey then at WXYZ radio. And standing there at the Walled Lake Casino, I was watching Jimmy McCarty, the guitar player for the Rivieras — he still has his band, Mystery Train, in Detroit today. Jimmy was playing an unprecedented rock and roll guitar, a hand-carved arch-top jazz guitar made by Gibson at the time called the Byrdland. It was that moment, when Jimmy was playing that Byrdland guitar, that inspired me to choose that same guitar, which has become my identity over the years. I'm the only guy since Jimmy who has ever used a Gibson Byrdland for rock and roll, because it was generally designed as a jazz instrument way back then.

This was the basic primal scream of rock and roll. Chuck Berry had just learned to turn the amp up, and become more obnoxious, and we were doing our damnedest to reproduce it.

We were basically in the vapor trail of Lewis & Clark of guitars at that point — Les Paul had basically just invented the damned thing, and the music was just starting to utilize it to any real dynamic. You had the Ventures, Dick Dale and the Del-Tones, Booker T and the MGs, and ultimately Elvis Presley and Chuck Berry and then the Stones and the Beatles. Of course, we know what happened after that. But that was a highly inspirational time. And I was fortunate to be in the eye of that sonic baptismal storm.

It was just such a moving experience because of the depth of virtuosity that all the members of Billy Lee and the Rivieras — all those band members — projected at that early stage of the game. It represented a dynamic convergence of all things musical for me, and I remember it like it was right now. It was very, very intriguing for a young kid like that to be exposed to such virtuosity. It was uninhibited creative juice flow to a white-water rapids degree. It was highly inspirational for me to hone my craft into and to dedicate my heart and soul to my musical vision. I think that had a lot to do with my constant and militant defiance of the drugs and alcohol in the music industry, that kept me bright-eyed and bushy-tailed throughout my life so I could somehow play that damned jazz instrument the way that Jimmy McCarty did. To this day he remains a friend and inspiration.

"

We were in musical cultivation and
idea exploratory mode. It was a very moving time,
and I'm just so pleased I had been born
at the right time to be there.

"

Marshall Fredericks was a sculptor.
Photographed at his studio on Woodward Avenue in Royal Oak.

I've been working here in Detroit since 1932, a long time. I was about 24 when I moved here. Life was much more slow and simpler, you know. Not so many cars, not so many people. It was very slow economically, too, with no opportunities for young people during the depression. People just did what they could to survive.

Before I came to Michigan, I did everything, I worked as a day laborer, as a waiter in a restaurant, I worked at a construction company. It was very, very hard — I could have stayed on that path, having nothing to do with art, except for the fact that my sister kept after me. She thought I had talent. She sort of forced me into art, but I'm glad she did.

I eventually went to art school in Cleveland. I was a good student, loved every minute of it. When I graduated, I won a traveling scholarship. I chose Sweden, because I had always wanted to go there. My ancestors were Scandinavian, and I had always been interested in the culture and in seeing the land. When I got there, I met the famous sculptor, Carl Milles. He was actually preparing to come here, to Detroit. But he spent time with me, and let me work in his studio — that's where I learned to do all this. Years later, he contacted me and offered me a job teaching at Cranbrook, which at the time was just getting started. He invited me to come work with him. He had commissions he wanted to do, and he wanted me to help him, to take some of the everyday teaching off his back. So I did. I taught there for 10 years, six days and two nights a week and also opened up my own studio.

Then the Japanese attacked Pearl Harbor. I was very loyal to this country, and I enlisted in the military, left Detroit and spent $3\frac{1}{2}$ years overseas. When I came back, I opened this studio on Woodward Avenue.

I enjoyed teaching, and I think I was pretty good at it. I knew my craft quite well. One thing I got out of the time I spent working in building and construction was the ability to work with my hands. I learned to use tools, and to use my hands to make things. And I guess that translates into making art. I always tried to pass that on to students, teaching them how to use the tools to make exactly what they envision. Lots of former students of mine write to me and thank me for it.

Bill Bonds is a nationally recognized news reporter and commentator.
Photographed at his home in Bloomfield Hills.

I have always been intrinsically curious, and when I look back to who the three most influential people in my life were, they stand out not just for what they have taught me, but I believe it's because I later found out they were very curious, too.

Curious people listen more, retain and then give back by communicating well, so that they give more of themselves than they're really asking for, but in the process they discover things of which other people are not aware; they have a dynamic force.

In my life, one of the three most influential people was a nun who taught my class in sixth grade — Sister Marilyn. She used to call me "Billy Why." In the sixth grade you were starting to get into algebra, Thomas Paine, James Madison, the Declaration of Independence, civics and government and wars. I could never go for 15 minutes without asking "why" about something. When you get a nun like Sister Marilyn, she loved it. One day, she asked, "Billy, why do you ask 'why' so much?"

I hesitated, then said, "Sister Marilyn, why do you ask?"

The class just went nuts. She came right down the aisle, gave me a kiss and said, "I don't know what I'd do without you. You have great communication skills, Billy, don't forget that."

The second person was a middle-aged Jewish guy, Mr. Goldberg. He lived right next door to me, which was at Burlingame and Twelfth Street, about seven blocks from where the '67 riots were.

Mr. Goldberg was an early riser. And he was a real curious guy. He used to be a trader, and every morning he would leave the house at about five o'clock. I used to be up at that time; I liked to be up early in the morning. He'd leave every morning and then he'd come home in a different car. He was very, very bright. He played the piano, played the violin, played chess, spoke nine languages, he was a cantor, and a wonderful, warm man.

One afternoon he came up in a green car, I was sitting there and I had my baseball mitt and my ball. "Billy boy, Billy boy, Bill," he said. "Why are you sitting there by yourself? What's wrong?"

"Well," I said, "that Steinberg guy, he won't let me play." Steinberg was a big kid, about three years older than me, and he would never let me play in the neighborhood ball games.

"Go on out there," Mr. Goldberg told me. "What do you want to play today?"

"I want to play shortstop."

"Then go play shortstop."

I said, "Mr. Goldberg, I can't; I'm afraid of him."

He said, "Go on over there. But when he pushes you, you pop him right in the nose. And I'll tell you why. What's the one thing a bully is afraid of? Now think about this, Billy."

And I thought about it. I finally said, "Somebody who's not afraid of him?"

He said, "You're right. They never get hit. Hit him. You know what will happen? His nose will bleed, he'll start crying, and he'll never pick on anybody again."

I never forgot that. And I think that was a great help to me in terms of my career. Interviewing people like Richard Nixon, Roger Smith or Lee Iacocca, I never was intimidated. I felt if I did my homework, I would stead well.

Finally, the third most influential person was my mother. She was a beautiful woman, born around the turn of the century, a gifted intellectual, very strong and a marvelous teacher. She would praise loudly and criticize softly. This is one of the great stories and occurrences in my life, one that I think had much to do with forming my values, growing up in a Jewish, Irish, Catholic neighborhood with a scattering of black children, and going to a Catholic school. My father was an outcast who just hated the church — they were always asking for money for the Catholic missions.

In the fifth grade, there were two black kids in our class — Margaret and Eddie. One day the nun said, "Boys and girls, tonight I want you to ask your parents for 25 cents; bring it in tomorrow for the little black babies over in Africa, so our missionaries can convert them to Catholics so they can go to heaven."

Later that same afternoon, the nun sent Margaret and Eddie out of the class to run an errand for Mother Superior. And while they were gone, she said to the class, "Boys and girls, you notice there are some black families moving in to the area from the east side. When you go home tonight, be sure to tell your parents that if one of those families moves onto your block, and if they ask about the Catholic school here, be sure your mother and father tell them we're all full, there's no room, because the bishop doesn't want any more black children in our school."

I knew my dad wasn't going to like having to give money for the missions, and my mother wasn't going to like the other part of it. As we were leaving, the nun said, "Remember the two things I told you to do — bring your 25 cents tomorrow, and remember what I told you about the kids coming to school." And of course, Margaret and Eddie hadn't heard the second part.

So I raised my hand. "Sister, are we supposed to ask our parents for the 25 cents for the black children in Africa before or after we tell our mom and dad the bishop doesn't want any more black kids in our school?" She went ballistic. I got kicked out of school and I couldn't come back until I came back with my mother and apologized to the nun and the rest of the class.

So I hid in the basement for two days.

Finally one night at dinner my brother said, "Mom, why don't you ask Bill what's wrong."

So I told her what happened. The next day, my mom took me to Mother Superior, who said, "Well, you know how Billy is, he's a hellion. He's going to have to apologize to the sister and apologize to the class."

My mother looked at her with her piercing blue eyes and said, "I want to hear your version of it. I don't get it, and he's not going to apologize. The nun's going to apologize. In front of the class. And if not, I will go to the chancellor — and my family is connected." Of course, we were broke, but we were connected.

And the Mother Superior asked, "Are you threatening me, Mrs. Bonds?"

My mother leaned across the table and said, "You're goddamn right I'm threatening you. This is hypocrisy and prejudice." The first thing I did when I got home was look up hypocrisy in the dictionary.

I love learning and I think life's greatest gift other than life is curiosity. Those three people helped me to understand myself, the rewards for not being afraid to risk things and not being afraid to stand up for what you think is right. And those are gifts that have lasted for a lifetime.

u

Curious people listen more, retain

and then give back by communicating well,

so that they give more of themselves than they're really asking for,

but in the process they discover things of which other people

are not aware; they have a dynamic force.

n

Elizabeth Berkley is an actress.
Photographed at the Four Seasons Hotel in Beverly Hills, California.

I love the Franklin Cider Mill. It was a beautiful place — kind of a magical place. As a child, just the smell of the donuts, the apples and the caramel made it one of my favorite activities. And its beautiful setting in Franklin made it such a tranquil spot.

Some of the best times in my childhood were spent there. To me, the Franklin Cider Mill was all about our family being together. It was always part of the fall time for us, and it was a beautiful part of my upbringing. Every once in a while, my parents would just say, "We're going to the cider mill," and it would be a nice surprise. They would take my older brother Jason and me there — sometimes my grandparents would come, too. My dad and I would always get the caramel apples. I always loved going there with my family. A few years ago, when I went back to visit my brother — he's doing his residency at Botsford now — we all went to the Franklin Cider Mill together again, and sat on the lawn on a blanket. We had a fun afternoon, and it brought back a lot of memories.

Even school provided me with some great Franklin Cider Mill memories — I went to Cranbrook's Kingswood Middle School, and on the day they had the boys' school and the girls' school meet, we met at the Franklin Cider Mill.

Whenever September or October rolls around, wherever I am, even in hot weather in sunny LA, I always remember the Franklin Cider Mill.

The Detroit area has so many wonderful memories for me. I loved Cranbrook. When I was little I went to Cranbrook Theatre school during the summer, and I enjoyed the Greek

Theatre where we would perform outside. And *The Nutcracker* ballet at Ford Auditorium was a holiday ritual for me. Every Christmas season growing up I did *The Nutcracker* at Ford Auditorium — we performed with the principal dancers from the New York City Ballet. I had a lot of wonderful teachers in Michigan, too — wonderful, nurturing, amazing, creative teachers who really prepared me so I was able to go out there and compete with the rest of them. A few of them were Barbara Fink — my first teacher for tap and jazz — Cheryl Sulek, and Iacob Lascu, who directed *The Nutcracker*. I'm really grateful for having had the opportunity to learn from them.

I grew up in Rolling Oaks subdivision in Farmington Hills — we lived in the same house my whole childhood. My favorite part of that house was the basement, because my parents had it finished, and they built a dance studio down there. It's not as glamorous as it sounds, but for me it was perfect. It was my rehearsal room — I worked so hard down there, practicing my singing and dancing and acting. I made it really special. It was very simple, with a barre and a mirror and the floor that was all scuffed up from my tap shoes. And I had a little spotlight in which I put a pink light bulb. That was my favorite room that I ever had. It's funny talking about this right now, sitting in the middle of the main flow of traffic in London. I'm here to do a play, and I'm talking about that little room where it all started. There is something very profound about that to me, kind of a reminder where it all started. So whatever little girl's in that house, I hope she's practicing, too.

I loved growing up in Michigan, and I'm so grateful that I grew up there, because it's enabled me to have wonderful, wonderful roots in a community that's about family and warm, warm people. It's something I carry with me always. No matter how tough the business sometimes can get, it's a foundation that forever will be with me.

Heinz C. Prechter is the Chairman and Founder of ASC Incorporated.
Photographed at ASC Headquarters in Southgate.

"You must be crazy! You want to do what? Cut a hole in the roof of this brand-new Cadillac? Get out o' here!"

These were the so-called good old days.

Before I came to Detroit in the late sixties, I sold a product virtually unknown in North America to car dealerships on the West Coast: sunroofs! Believe me, it was a tough sell for a little fellow with a big toolbox and a heavy German accent. I had left home at the age of thirteen. Home was a small farming village in southern Germany. Not wanting to be a farmer, I became an apprentice in automotive coach-building and interior trim in the city of Nuremberg. My restlessness eventually led me to San Francisco as an exchange student. And to make some money on the side I did what I did best: install sunroofs. I opened my own business in a two-car garage annexed to legendary George Barris' Kustom Car City and called it the American Sunroof Company. I spent $764 on tools, a workbench from an old door covered with aluminum and a sewing machine from a junkyard. Now I was selling sunroofs by day and installed them at night, sometimes pulling in strangers who walked by my shop to hold my measuring tape so I could find the midpoint on the car's roof.

I also worked on custom-made cars for Hollywood's stars like Steve McQueen, James Garner, and, later on, Frank Sinatra, which drew the attention of the big players in the automotive industry. Ford Motor Company took notice and after John F. Kennedy was tragically shot while driving in his open-air car, brought me in to design an open-air system on President Johnson's limousine, which would also serve as a shield to protect him. In the process, Henry Ford II took a liking to me, this young German mechanic.

It was Ford Motor Company that invited me to come to Detroit in the first place. Tom Denomme, who retired in 1998 as Vice Chairman of Chrysler, was a young product planning manager at Ford back then. He first discovered what I was doing on the West Coast (thank you, Tom). After doing sample sunroof installations on five Thunderbirds, I got my first big break in 1968. ASC launched its first major program installing 500 electrically powered sunroofs in the Mercury Cougar XR7. Unfortunately, that project was interrupted by a strike. So I went to Chrysler and started a program with the 1968 Charger. And from there I went to General Motors and convinced Cadillac to have sunroofs. With the Big Three as my customers, ASC prospered. My first shop was in a rough ethnic neighborhood at 115 Southfield Road in Ecorse. Detroit was going through a very difficult time with the riots clearly on the horizon. I remember armored vehicles patrolling the streets. There was a curfew in effect to prevent angry Detroiters to march on "posh" downriver neighborhoods.

Outgrowing its quarters, ASC moved to the Technical Center in Southgate. And guess what? We expanded the Tech Center every six months. Life was good, until . . . I nearly lost everything! The oil crisis of 1979 virtually shut down the luxury car market ASC catered to. The crash almost wiped out everything I had worked for, forcing me to lay off seven out of ten employees. That was one of the most painful decisions I ever had to make in my life. I was devastated, but quitting was not an option. I rebuilt ASC and turned it into the leading company it is today — for a second time.

Only the Motor City offered me the opportunity to live my dream many times over. Looking back, I'm sure glad I left sunny California for Detroit.

Gregory J. Reed is an attorney and author.
Photographed at the Charles H. Wright Museum of African American History in Detroit.

ANGELS OF DETROIT

Growing up and living in Detroit has been a journey of cultural enrichment made possible by angels who have been willing to guide me from time to time or pass the baton that has allowed me to run the race. These angels have prepared me for many encounters near and far, but especially in Detroit. The city has so much to offer African-Americans when we give it a chance and get involved at whatever level, despite the obstacles every human will encounter due to the small-mindedness that exists in all races of people.

One of the first angels I met, besides my mother, was a high school counselor at Southwestern High School named Ms. Alma Whittley. She had a reputation as a hard, strict disciplinarian. To avoid encountering her, I went to Chadsey High School. After I was enrolled there for one half of a semester, I got so lonely for my neighborhood friends that I enrolled in my designated school, Southwestern. I felt I had maneuvered and tricked the system to avoid being under the heavy-handedness of Ms. Alma Whittley. On my very first day of school after transferring to Southwestern, I walked right into Ms. Whittley in the principal's office. Not knowing that all students are assigned alphabetically by their last name, I immediately discovered that I was one of her students! She looked me in the face and said, "You're going to give me all As and Bs and Cs and no babies." By her guidance, I became one of the Detroit Public Schools' National Merit Scholars and class president, among other honors. She became my angel of guidance and led me to Michigan State University, her second choice over Hampton University. She helped many others to realize their life goals as well, such as Dr. Ben Carson, the internationally renowned surgeon, who was a sophomore at Southwestern when I was a senior.

From that beginning, Detroit angels came to me more often in all forms and colors because I was open to growth and change. At Michigan State University, two Detroiters shaped my direction: Professor Harry Stephens, who had gone to Eastern High School, and Dr. Robert Green, an activist who had ties to Martin Luther King, Jr. Dr. Green molded me in a way that taught me to enter the race of life as a participant and not as someone sitting on the sidelines. Because of this encouragement, I have made many friendships from around the country and across the globe while nurturing lifelong Detroit relationships.

One day at Michigan State University, Green told me I should meet a man named Coleman Alexander Young in the Michigan Senate. Green stated that Coleman Young would one day be a great leader and he would need supporters like me. He sent me over to see Young, who welcomed me with open arms and informed me of his vision to be the first African-American mayor of Detroit. He said, "I want you on board before I run." This was all new to me. I got on board as one of his researchers, never knowing history was in the making!

After I left Michigan State and entered law school, I got a job interview letter from the law firm of Goodman, Eden, Millender and Bedrosian, the first integrated law firm in the nation. They were interested in me because of my undergraduate engineering degree with a background in law. The letter came from Mr. Bedrosian who was in trial. I did not know lawyers had such busy schedules. I thought they talked on the phone with their feet on the desk most of the time. This was before we had television shows such as *L.A. Law* or *Perry Mason*. Two to three weeks went by and I never heard from the firm. I went up to the firm and sort of demanded to see Mr. Bedrosian. The secretary did not know what to do; she called Mr. Robert Millender, "the political king maker." Mr. Millender came out of his office to see me. I did not know who he was and did not care, I needed a job. I never knew he was the angel who would guide Coleman A. Young, Erma Henderson (the first councilwoman to chair the Detroit City Council), Congressman John Conyers, Secretary of State Richard Austin and many others destined to be prominent or the first in their professional positions.

Mr. Millender questioned me on the law a great deal to see how sharp and smart I was. I had an answer for every question, and then I got impatient with this technique. I hit his desk with my fist and said, "I need a job and I'm a hustler!" (This was a positive expression before movers and shakers was contrived.) He put down his cigar and said, "Reed, I know what you mean; I am a hustler, too. All of our positions are filled and Mr. Bedrosian is in a trial. I don't want to hold you any longer at our office. I will send you to a white firm that has never hired an African-American law clerk: Ripple, Chambers and Steiner. If you get in, you will know what to do — do a good job! Tell them I sent you." I went there and all eyes were dilated. I told them that Bob Millender sent me. The next words out of the managing partner's mouth were, "When do you want to start?" Mr. Millender became another angel of guidance in my life. Today we have the Millender Center, across from the Renaissance Center, as a monument to his impact upon this city.

Detroit has had so many angels, leaders and supporters who were great warriors and doers that prepared many of us. I have learned that if you are sincere and want to do something worthwhile, Detroit has angels who will help you.

One other great person — a saint above all angels — who prepared me to be humble in all of my affairs was Mrs. Rosa Parks, Mother of our Nation, not just of the civil rights movement. Her influence enabled me to minister to Dr. Betty Shabazz when I recovered the *Malcolm X* manuscript and unpublished chapters from the estate of Alex Haley. Mrs. Parks' spirit also enabled me to author the following words when we were writing *Quiet Strength,* the book Congresswoman Julia Carson stated inspired her to launch the drive to present the Congressional Medal of Honor to Mrs. Parks. (The book also outsold the Bible for 30 days and is quoted in the Women's Devotional Bible.)

"My message to Detroit and to the world is we must come together and live as one. There is only one world; and yet we, as a people, have treated the world as if it were divided. We cannot allow the gains we have made to erode. Although we have a long way to go, I do believe that we can achieve Dr. King's dream of a better world. From time to time I catch a glimpse of that world. I can see a world where children do not learn hatred in their homes. I can see a world where mothers and fathers have the last and most important word. I can see a world in which all adults protect the innocence of children. I can see a world in which people do not call each other names based on skin color. I can see a world free of acts of violence. I can see a world in which people of all races and all religions work together to improve the quality of life for everyone. I can see this world because it exists today in small pockets of this country and in a small pocket of every person's heart. If we will look to God and work together — not only here but everywhere — then others will see this world too and help to make it a reality."

I am glad to be a Detroiter, and I am thankful that God has placed me in the midst of so many wonderful angels!

"

I hit his desk with my fist and said,

'I need a job and I'm a hustler!'

"

Norbert Schemansky has received medals in four consecutive Olympic Games and set 27 world records in weightlifting.

Photographed at his home in Dearborn.

I grew up on the east side, Harper and Van Dyke area. All the neighborhoods were separate then. You had a Polish neighborhood, a German neighborhood, Harper and Gratiot was Italian — everybody was clustered. Even the churches. Italians went to one, Polish went to another. Every little area was a miniature city; each neighborhood seemed to have a five and dime, drug store, furniture store and a theater. At Harper and Van Dyke was the Eastown Theater. Harper and Gratiot had Roosevelt Theater. Now, everything's at the malls. We'd play baseball and football right out in the street or in the alley. When I was about 18, going into the Army, I told the recruiter I could throw a football 70 yards. The guy asked me, how do you know you can throw the ball 70 yards? Because I could throw it seven houses. Lots were 30 feet. 10 yards.

I was 13 when I first started training. My older brother, Dennis, was a weightlifter. I kind of looked up to him, so I tagged along to try it out. I'd wait until the older guys were taking showers, getting dressed and stuff like that, then I started puttering around with the weights. I'd wait because the older guys didn't want this kid fooling around in between them. I was just a punk, but pretty soon, I was doing more than the guys who were training regularly. I got hooked. I went roughly three or four times a week, mostly in the evenings. The "gym" was a garage on McClellan near Gratiot. Right now it would be in the middle of the expressway. It was a wooden garage; these guys boarded up the inside, fixed it up, put a heater in there, and a shower. Sometimes the heater didn't work. At that time, working out wasn't popular like it is today. People would see you walking down the street with your gym bag and they'd ask, "Where are you going?" I'd say, "To work out;" they'd say, "Go get a job!" They didn't have gyms like we've got now. In fact, if somebody knew you were training then and lifting weights, you were nuts. Now everybody's nuts.

Later on, I started going to the YMCA at Harper and Gratiot. I used to sneak in there to train; I didn't have the money to pay for it. I got to know the guy who opened the door, so he'd just let me in. I used to sneak in there so much that the Athletic Director thought I was a regular member. And he never questioned me. They had about twenty guys working out in one little 10-by-12 room. Think about that compared to what the gyms are like now. The equipment was shot — bars were bent, you'd have to try to straighten them out. When you're hooked, you're hooked, I guess. Training wasn't like you see Olympic guys training now (they're all over-trained anyway). Between my house and the YMCA was a pool hall. So I'd usually run to the gym (about a mile), I'd see someone in the pool hall, stop in and shoot a few games of pool, then go work out. I think guys a long time ago could do better because they were just more relaxed. In one contest at that YMCA, the record was 341. I took 343 and missed it; so I took 349 and made it. The AAU officials weren't there, so I didn't get credit for it. So a couple weeks later, I went to Baltimore and did 351 — more yet. I went there because it was a sanctioned meet. That was the way you had to do things.

I never had a trainer — we had some guys, they'd know every bean they ate. The AAU people used to run all the sports then; they used to get mad at me — they said I was a bad example for the kids because I ate hamburgers, pizza, drank beer. Everything you're not supposed to — the opposite of good training. The other guys ate steaks, drank milk — they'd worry so much about what they were eating, it affected their training. They said I had a bad attitude. I said, "My attitude is winning."

I just wanted to do more, that's all. There were certain guys around the country who were good; you'd try to keep tabs on them. If you had a ten-pound lead on a guy, you were good enough to beat him for a year.

After the war, I trained at a Naval Base at Mellon and Schaefer. It's not there now. They had a big gym, mostly a basketball court; the weightlifting and wrestling was down in the basement, in a cage. I had to bring my own weights down there. I left them there as long as they would let me train there, until they got ready to tear it down and I had to find a new place to train.

One of the first private gyms around was Yacos Gym; they opened in 1948 or 1950. It was at the Taft Hotel just off of Mack and Woodward. The gym was an old dining room. The dining room was vacated, so he took that over. That was halfway decent, the beginning of what gyms are now. George, the owner, let me train for nothing because I used to represent him at the contest, but training dues would have been between $5 and $10 a month. The other gym that opened back then was Armentos Gym at Seven Mile and Woodward. Most of the weightlifting was done at Yacos, though. He had more weights than anybody; he had graduated weights all around the place.

I went to the White House twice. The first time was when Eisenhower was in office; he had all the sports champions from the year before there. The temperature was 90, the humidity was 90, no air conditioning in the White House. So all these sports guys show up, and they're all dressed up, jackets, ties and all that. I show up in a polo shirt. They had us all lined up, all these guys are dressed up. Archie Moore, the boxer, was standing next to me. Eisenhower looks at me and says, "Looks like you're the smartest one here." Everyone else was sweating like crazy. Archie started laughing. By the time we ate, everyone had their coats on the chairs.

The second time was Johnson. Kind of the same thing, everybody had to introduce themselves. "What sport are you in?" "Weightlifting," I said. He said, "Looks like we're the two strongest Democrats around."

"

Between my house and the YMCA was a pool hall.

So I'd usually run to the gym (about a mile), I'd see someone in the pool hall,

stop in and shoot a few games of pool, then go work out.

I think guys a long time ago could do better because they were just more relaxed.

"

Jerry Linenger is an astronaut and author.

Photographed in Suttons Bay.

Early on during my mission aboard the Russian space station Mir, I decided that I would be a good father and write daily letters to my then 14-month-old son, John. Of course, I knew that he would not be able to read them for quite some time. But I wanted him to have the letters so that later in his life he would know that his father was thinking about him while traveling in space for nearly five months.

My space mission did not go as planned. After a relatively calm first month on Mir, a raging fire broke out. The fire burned uncontrollably for fourteen minutes, with three-foot flames roaring out of a solid-fueled oxygen generator. Choking smoke filled every nook and cranny of the station. The first respirator I donned failed. Desperate for air, I flung it off, and feeling my way along a bulkhead — the smoke so dense that it was impossible to see — I was able to locate a second one by touch. Realizing that this was my last hope, I put the rubber mask over my head, threw the activation lever, and breathed in deeply and desperately. Oxygen flowed.

Recovered from near air starvation, I told myself that "We need to fight this fire, we need to get the fire out. We are trapped with nowhere to go. No mistakes, Jerry."

Amidst the smoke, the thought that I could die also crossed my mind, I said aloud to no one: "Kathryn (my wife), I love you. Take care of John and our child-to-be. I will give it everything that I have to survive. I am sorry if I let you down." I was not at all certain that it would be humanly possible to overcome the odds against us.

After some terrifying moments, we finally put the fire out. Having beaten the odds, it was great to be able to continue writing to John. The experience of the fire probably helped me open up to him a bit more, to let my guard down. The fire made me realize that at any point in any of our lives, very abruptly it could be all over. The fire was a stark reminder that life is precarious and that I was living on the edge, out on the frontier. "Why hold anything back from my son?" I thought to myself. "Tell him how much I love him. Try to convey to him what I consider important in life and what his father stands for. Try to tell him of the hopes and dreams that I have for him — before it is too late." My guard down, I began to write from the heart.

The letters often talked of Michigan. Of how, for example, I had taught my cosmonaut crewmates only one word of English, the word, "Michigan." Flying over the hand print of Michigan … Michigan does indeed look like a mitten from space … Vasily and Sasha would yell, "Jerry, Meeshegan! Meeshegan!" Looking broadly, I could see the curvature of the earth and mainland United States in one glance. Looking down hard, I could make out the Mackinac Bridge. I could even see I-75 appearing as a dark line as it weaved its way out of Detroit past the snow-covered landscape. Squinting through a 250mm camera, I could make out Gratiot and Woodward, and could even imagine, at least, seeing my house in Eastpointe! "Hi Mom," I would say to no one as we flew past at 18,000 mph.

The following is one such letter that I wrote to my son, John, from space.

7 April 1997.

NEVER LOOK AT LASERS.

Dear John:

I received a note the other day from my former high school swimming coach Dave Clark. He is not the bandstand guy (his name was Dick Clark) nor part of the Dave Clark Five rock group that no one really cared for because they merely copied the beloved Beatles. Coach Clark was a teacher at East Detroit High School.

He wrote that people were pulling for me, thinking of me, worry over me, and proud of me back on planet earth. That comment made me feel good inside and I worked even harder than usual today. Perhaps the sound of his name evoked a potential across a memory nerve inside my brain, activating my recall of the sound of his whistle blaring and of him yelling. "Pick it up, sprint, no breathing, go!" He always pushed us hardest when our arms already felt like lead and our lungs were about to burst. Although not pleasant at the time, his prodding taught me the lesson that no matter how tired I became, no matter how much I thought that I had reached my limit, it was still possible to reach down inside further yet and find more energy. To tap into some hidden reserve and persist. It was a valuable lesson learned.

He also spoke of family. How all parents feel the same way that I do; with an almost magical love of their children.

Mommy says that you are a smart little guy. I, of course, agree. But what parent doesn't feel that about their child? While all children are special, our own children, when viewed from through the lens of parental eyes, become extra, extra special. I hope that you feel secure knowing that to Mommy and me, you are the most important, loved person in the world. An extension of the love that we have for each other.

Wow! How is that for a Dad showing his soft side?

In the space business, it has once again been a busy day. Measuring diffusion coefficients in metals. Tracking my biorhythms. Recording radiation levels. Examining microbes on Petri dishes. Checking crew health. Looking ahead and reviewing contingency procedures for the planned Progress re-supply vehicle docking tomorrow.

In spite of the heavy workload, I did find time to glance out the window as we passed overhead the Amazon. Sadly, I saw smoke plume after smoke plume rising into the atmosphere from fires burning below. The fires are being intentionally lit in order to clear-cut the jungle for farming. The people on the ground probably do not realize the extent of the damage that they are causing. The view from space makes it all too clear.

Japan at night was once again spectacular. The entire coastline was aglow from the lights of towns and cities, with Tokyo shining as brightly and over as wide an area as any city on earth.

One place that I will not be looking down at is France. They will be conducting a tracking experiment tonight, attempting to aim a laser at us as we zoom by them. It is wise not to put one's retina in the path of a laser beam. There is a new one to add to your list of do's and don'ts, John; right after "Don't bite other peoples legs," add "Never look at lasers out the windows of spacecraft." I know that it must be difficult keeping track of all these do's and don'ts!

I hope that you had another adventurous, learning day yourself, John.

Goodnight. Pleasant dreams. Love you.

Dad.

"

I could see the curvature of the earth and mainland United States in one glance.

Looking down hard, I could make out the Mackinac Bridge.

I could even see I-75 appearing as a dark line as it weaved its way

out of Detroit past the snow-covered landscape.

"

Neeme Järvi is Music Director of the Detroit Symphony Orchestra.
Photographed at Orchestra Hall in Detroit.

It was Saturday afternoon, May 31, in 1997. As I made my way from my home, near Lake St. Clair, to Orchestra Hall, I knew it was going to be a memorable night. This was the final weekend of the 1996-1997 season and I knew the staff was also planning a celebration of my 60th birthday (my actual birthdate is June 7). As I looked back on what was, at the time, my seventh year as music director of the Detroit Symphony Orchestra, I was pleased and surprised at how comfortable this city had come to feel as my second home. This orchestra is warm, enthusiastic and inspiring to me. My home near the lake reminds me of Estonia's beautiful shores and makes me feel as though I'm in the presence of an old friend. When I arrived at Orchestra Hall that Saturday, waiting for me were birthday greetings from many friends — Itzhak Perlman, Isaac Stern, Eddie Daniels, Jimmy DePriest, Msislav Rostropovich … even the president of Estonia, Lennart Meri.

At rehearsal, the orchestra surprised me by playing the Estonian version of "Happy Birthday," a piece called Ta Elagu (which means congratulations in Estonian).

The concert series that weekend featured the "Rock" Symphony by Latvian composer Imant Kalnins, and that was the first time an American audience had ever heard his music. In fact, this concert series was also the first time Kalnins himself had ever heard his symphony the way he intended it — Latvian authorities did not approve of the poetry lyrics and stripped them away before the first performance was given and before any recordings could be made. I can well remember what it was like for artists in my native Estonia and in former Soviet Union under the communist regime. There was no tolerance for artistic expression unless it was approved by the party. So this was truly an historic weekend.

Saturday night's performance was spectacular. When I gave the opening downbeat, instead of playing my fellow Estonian Heino Eller's "Song of My Homeland" as I expected, the Orchestra played "Happy Birthday" (the American version this time). The audience thought that was just great. As the concert continued, I'll never forget the passion with which the orchestra played. And when it came time for the finale, I watched with pride as my son, Kristjan, stepped out to conduct Stravinsky's "Greeting Prelude."

I grew up in a home where music was the focus, and each of our children has also pursued a life and career in music. It is a pleasure also to be a part of a city where music plays an important role. To me, the music and the warmth of the people here are the best things about Detroit.

Neal Shine is the retired publisher of the Detroit Free Press and currently a professor of journalism.
Photographed at Fifth Avenue Billiards in Royal Oak.

Whatever else it might have been, to us it was simply the neighborhood.

If it had any corporate boundaries, nobody ever told us exactly what they were. I suppose we might have told anybody who insisted that it ran from around Water Works Park on the west, probably to the railroad tracks by the Chrysler plant on the east, to Mack Avenue on the north, and south to the Detroit River.

But whatever geographic limits we assigned those blocks, it was the place that defined our existence. The place where we lived, where we grew up. Where we were nurtured by the people who lived there and shaped by its institutions — church, school and, for me and for what seemed like most of my friends, the poolroom.

I still believe that the social history of Detroit is richer for the existence in this city of that often maligned and misunderstood institution.

When I was growing up in Detroit in the 1930s and 1940s, poolrooms had unenviable reputations as places where all manner of nefarious activity thrived.

They were characterized as venal places harboring the city's misfits. Idlers who lay in wait for unsuspecting youth in order to turn them from productive pursuits into the kind of persons universally scorned by society. Loafers.

In a 1926 story on page one of *The Detroit Free Press,* readers were warned of the dangers lurking within the smoky confines of the city's poolrooms. One person called them "cesspools of crime" and "a meeting place of loafers and young rascals, experimentalists in petty crime."

Today's parents concerned about the behavioral well-being of their children sometimes tend to compare video arcades to the poolrooms of old as places where bad habits abound and where their children might succumb to the temptation to become, well, loafers.

I think the comparison fails.

Places like video arcades, where the air is split with the piercing and undulating sounds of electronic conflict, will never produce any really memorable loafers. People locked to the controls of a machine, eyes frozen by exploding images on a screen, trying to repel invaders of the evil Gorfian robot empire, do not have the stuff of which great loungers are made.

Effective loafing requires, most of all, atmosphere. Lassitude must be nurtured in languorous, almost somnolent surroundings, which the video arcade will never provide.

Detroit's poolrooms, I always feel compelled to defend the place where I learned a lot about life. Despite the seediness of its surroundings — and many of its clientele — the poolroom had its own quiet dignity and a standard of etiquette that went quite beyond the posted prohibitions against gambling, loitering, swearing, roughhousing and spitting anywhere except in vessels provided for that purpose.

Over the years I have watched my children and grandchildren use laser cannons to scatter electronic fragments of make-believe villains across glass galaxies. At the controls of Space Invader, Armor Attack, Spectar, Gorf, Space Zap, Berzerk and Galaxian, they disintegrated little green blips at 25 cents per space war.

It's good for them, I told myself. It's a computer world and it gives them a head start in that kind of technology. It's also good, they say, for hand-eye coordination. What good, I ask myself, has my ability to sink a straight-rail shot ever been to me in my life?

I still find myself wishing I could have convinced my mother in those years that snooker improved hand-eye coordination.

For one thing, I would not have had to spend all that time brushing chalk off my clothes before I went home.

For example, there was never any loud talking when someone was lining up a shot. No squeaky chalking of cue tips. No coughs or throat-clearing. Some quiet observations were allowed, however, but were generally limited to such undisputed statements of fact as, "That's a lot of green, Eddie."

The lighting was always, in a word, subdued. Green-shaded lights hung low over the green baize surface of each pool table, enabling you to identify the persons you were playing with only by the color of their trousers or the recognition of a disembodied voice that would say quietly from beyond the light, "Didn't leave you much."

The poolroom responsible for at least part of my character formation was known in its various incarnations through the years as Tiny's, Harp's and Fleming's, the names of its owners. It was on Kercheval near Fairview, but exists now only in neighborhood lore. It was replaced by a VFW post, and later by the New Greater Whole Truth Temple, proving that it is possible to superimpose sanctity on premises where it had previously been in very short supply.

"

… the poolroom had its own quiet dignity

and a standard of etiquette that went quite beyond the posted prohibitions

against gambling, loitering, swearing, roughhousing and spitting anywhere

except in vessels provided for that purpose.

"

Selma Blair is an actress.

Photographed at Cranbrook in Bloomfield Hills.

Cranbrook was someplace completely out of time. It's a setting that could be anywhere … London … out east … it felt incredibly romantic to me, especially in my freshman year. Before that I had just gone to a tiny private school, so coming to Cranbrook I was so excited to be with people older than I was, at a place that had property and tennis courts and baseball fields. I was captivated, I couldn't believe I was a part of it.

There was a Greek theater there, off in the woods. At night I'd sneak my way out along with some of the boarders, we'd go there with our flashlights to sit and tell ghost stories, or put on little plays. That's when I realized I wanted to be an actress. There's a Zeus statue there, a big stone sculpture, and if you stand in front of it, it cries. There was a big hill there, too, that we used to go sliding down on — Wood Chip Hill, we called it. I got a concussion once trying to show off. I never wanted to leave Cranbrook. In fact I think I tried to fail out my first year so I could be held back — I was so busy checking everything out I forgot to do my schoolwork. And Cranbrook is where I got to know Chip — I was so in love with that boy. And with his family. His dad was like a dad to me, he was great … an amazing person. He loved Detroit more than anything — he was always into everything that was going on there.

During the summer of 1988 I was 15, and it was shortly before the Grand Prix. One night Chip's dad came home and told us we would all get to ride in the Grand Prix pace car. He was a vice president of Volkswagen of America, and was also an amateur race car driver. I was so excited, because I'd never been allowed to drive over 30 miles an hour. (My mom, she's very careful.) Also, we were living in Southfield, but we spent so much time in Detroit, my mom would never put up with driving down there on the most busy weekend — no way. So I got all dressed up, and we got in the pace car — Chip and I, with his dad at the wheel. And of course the pace car goes before all the other cars go off, it runs along the track. So we're driving around, Chip's dad was so thrilled, and the energy was so high. And all of a sudden, the energy gets a little higher. We suddenly saw everyone along the sidelines frantically removing tires and flagging us off. We had missed the turn, where we were supposed to exit the track — the Grand Prix race had begun, the cars were hurtling at us and we were still on the track. There we are in this little Volkswagen station wagon with a souped-up engine, on the same track as the Grand Prix cars. I had no idea. It could have been the end of our lives so quickly. But I'd do it again … I'd do it again! Chip and I stayed together for a long time after that — we had a bond. He's a part of all my best Detroit memories, that boy.

Steve Yzerman is captain of the Detroit Red Wings.
Photographed at Joe Louis Arena in Detroit.

Our locker room was deadly silent before the game. It was Saturday evening, June 7, 1997, Game Four of the playoffs. We had stayed at the Atheneum the night before the game, so we drove over to the rink from there at around 5:00. Already people were lined up outside the hotel; Red Wings stuff was everywhere we looked. It took quite a while to drive over to the Joe Louis Arena, because the streets were just filled with people in red and white — and when we got into the rink there was a whole gauntlet of people chanting. The game didn't start until 8:00, and with all the crowds of people, it was really exciting. The only trouble was, three hours before the game we were ready to go, and that's just not a good thing to be, in an important game when you're really anxious. So we were quiet in the locker room.

I remember the whole game that night. We really didn't play that well, because we were so nervous. We were up 3-0 in the series against the Flyers, but we were more nervous during that game than any other game in the playoffs by far. Fortunately, Nick Lidstrom scored in the first period, and I think everybody just breathed a big sigh of relief. And midway through the second, Darren McCarty scored on an end-to-end rush a beautiful goal, a highlight goal, and that proved to be the winner. Then the Flyers scored in the last thirty seconds in the game to make it 2-1. The whole building was going wild, and when the Flyers scored everybody just kind of gasped, so there was a lot of tension that last 15 or 20 seconds. Anyway, the game ended and everybody went wild. It was awesome. Streamers came down from the ceiling, and they played that song "Oh What A Night". I don't know if you'd call that a great song, but it is now, to me. It was just amazing.

Then I saw the Stanley Cup. They brought it out through the doors onto the ice. We were all around the blue line, and when people saw them bringing the thing out, the whole building, which was loud anyway, gave an extra roar. The whole building and the whole team. In some ways the experience was like the expectation of the birth of your child. You know it's coming, you're waiting for it. It's the same kind of feeling. I think the Cup weighs 35 pounds. At first it felt light, but we did a lap in the rink with it, and by the time I got $^2/_3$ of the way around, it was starting to feel pretty heavy. Holding the Stanley Cup is a proud time, because you've worked for it not just professionally, but your whole life playing hockey, and it's kind of a dream, getting the chance to win it one day. It was so rewarding, about as good a feeling you can have as a hockey player. That's the one thing that really matters, so it's a tremendous accomplishment.

We stayed out on the ice, everybody did a lap with the trophy, and it was awesome. We didn't leave the rink until about 3:30 in the morning. Everything just took a while. I don't know what time the game ended exactly, probably about 11:30. Then there was the celebration in the locker room, talking to the media and friends. By the time we got out of the locker room it was 1:30 or 2:00. The Ilitches were still up in their suite, so we went up there before leaving the rink and then finally made it out. I could have stayed there all night long. From there we all went out to a party at Big Daddy's in West Bloomfield, and we stayed there 'til about 5:30 or so.

The whole time was exciting — the playoff run leading up to the finals, and then the celebrations following, the parades and rallies, just the excitement of being around the city was amazing. That night has been the highlight of my seventeen years here so far. If you want to talk about one moment of my career, that's the ultimate one. That was the best day, the most exciting day, the most memorable day of my career, start to finish.

Elizabeth Berkley began performing as a child — she landed roles in equity theater productions by the age of nine. She won a regular role as Jesse in the instant teen hit *Saved By The Bell,* where she remained for three seasons and 100 episodes. She went on to win the lead role in her debut film, *Showgirls.* She then landed a memorable role in *The First Wives Club* opposite Goldie Hawn, Bette Midler and Diane Keaton. Berkley was chosen to star in Oliver Stone's *Any Given Sunday* opposite Al Pacino, and two independent features, *The Taxman* and *Last Call.* Berkley also starred in the London West End production of *Lenny* opposite British actor Eddie Izzard.

Selma Blair, a Detroit native, is rapidly becoming one of Hollywood's most sought-after young actresses. Currently she can be seen in the starring role in the WB series, *Zoe,* which follows the lives of a group of teens in New York City as they begin to find their places in the world. She also plays Cecile in the feature film *Cruel Intentions,* with Sarah Michelle Gellar, Ryan Phillippe and Reese Witherspoon. Other feature film roles include *Down To You* and lead roles in the independent films *Girl* and *Brown's Requiem.* Upcoming films include *A Leonard Cohen Afterworld, Trip* (a film about a girl from Michigan) and *Take My Life.* After graduating from high school, Blair planned to become a photographer. She moved to New York City to pursue her goal but found her way to acting classes, and was discovered by an agent in her class.

Bill Bonds has been the commentator on WXYZ-TV/Channel 7 since 1988. In the book, *The Newscasters,* Pulitzer Prize-winning television critic Ron Powers called him one of the six most influential news anchors in the country. From 1984 to 1988 he hosted a morning radio talk show on WXYT-AM and a late-night talk program on WJBK-TV/Channel 2. Prior to that, Bonds spent nearly 30 years at Channel 7. He was a news anchor for the 5 p.m. and 11 p.m. newscasts and also served as host of *Special Report,* which won Emmy Awards for Best Public Affairs Program and Best Magazine Format Program. Bonds has also anchored for ABC stations in Los Angeles and New York, as well as the ABC national weekend news. Bonds has also worked as a reporter for several Detroit radio stations, including WKNR and WCAR. He is a graduate of the University of Detroit, has completed graduate work at the University of Michigan and currently resides in Oakland County with his wife, Karen.

Pablo Bonilla was raised in Southwest Detroit. At the age of 15 or 16, he joined a gang called the Detroit Kings. Bonilla became the leader and the gang grew to nearly 170 members throughout the Detroit area and Toledo. Bonilla was eventually put in prison, where he spent nearly 18 months. Upon his release, he was contacted by Alex Montaner, founder and director of the GRACE program (Gang Retirement and Continued Education). The program teaches teens how to write a resume, interview for jobs, find work and other important skills. Bonilla completed the program and withdrew from gang life, got married and has worked his way up to a position as production and shipping and receiving manager at Munoz Machine. In addition to working full-time, he is involved in community outreach programs.

Jim Brandstatter, a lifelong Michigan resident, attended University of Michigan. He played football for Bo Schembechler and was named All

Big Ten his senior year, played for two Big Ten Championships and participated in two Rose Bowls. After his graduation in 1972, he began working as Sports Director at WEYI-TV in Saginaw. In 1975 he moved to WILX-TV in Lansing/Jackson and met news anchor Robbie Timmons, whom he later married in 1980. In 1977 Brandstatter moved to Detroit as a sports producer at WDIV-TV; he also hosted the Detroit Tigers network pre-game show for a year. In 1983 he moved to the freelance market; he has co-hosted *Michigan Replay, the Reebok Lions Report,* and served as talent and associate producer for the *Michigan Open Golf Championship* and the Emmy-nominated *Michigan Bell Showdown.* He is color analyst for University of Michigan football on WJR and One on One Sports national radio network, and the color analyst voice on WXYT Lions football network. He also continues as host for *Michigan Replay* on WWJ-TV.

Dave Coulier was born in Detroit and raised in St. Clair Shores. An avid sportsman, he excelled in ice hockey, water skiing and swimming. He became interested in show business after he discovered he had a knack for impersonations and creating unusual voices. After amusing his friends throughout high school, Coulier began to hone his comedic skills in local Detroit clubs before moving to Los Angeles in 1979. He then began performing at The Comedy Store in Hollywood and built a repertoire that enabled him to feature his talents on such shows as *Showtime Laugh-a-Thon, Evening* at the Improv and HBO's *Detroit Comedy Jam.* In 1982, he made his film debut in the Cheech & Chong movie *Things are Tough All Over.* As a result of a brief stint on *The Tonight Show,* he was invited to appear on the comedy series *Family Ties* and *Newhart.* He has also performed several voices for characters on such popular morning cartoons as *Scooby Doo, Mork and Mindy, The Jetsons* and *The Real Ghostbusters.* He also won an Emmy® for his work on the cartoon series Jim Henson's *Muppet Babies.*

Mort Crim has over 30 years of broadcasting experience and is the creator and voice of the award-winning radio series *Second Thoughts,* airing on over 800 radio stations worldwide. For five years, he was the national correspondent for ABC; his voice described Neil Armstrong's landing on the moon for the national ABC radio audience. In the 1970s, his nationally syndicated series, *One Moment Please,* aired on more than 350 radio stations. In 1995 he was awarded the Gold World Medal as Best Radio Personality at the New York Festivals International Radio Awards, and the following year received the Festival's Silver Medal for Best Humor Writing. Crim is the author of three books: *One Moment Please, Like It Is* and *Second Thoughts: One Hundred Upbeat Messages for Beat-Up Americans.* He was Senior Editor and Anchor of the evening news at WDIV-TV in Detroit from 1978 to 1997 and continues to serve as WDIV's Vice President, Community Affairs. He serves on the Board of Directors of the Karmanos Cancer Institute, Alma College, Junior Achievement and the Michigan Thanksgiving Day Parade. He is currently Chairman, President and CEO of Mort Crim Communications, and he is a commercial licensed pilot. He and his wife, the former Irene (Renee) Bowman Miller, reside in Waterford, Michigan and Amelia Island, Florida.

Jeff Daniels has been a professional stage and film actor for 22 years. Raised in Michigan, Daniels attended Central Michigan University.

Marshall W. Mason invited him to join the Circle Repertory Company and Daniels accepted, leaving college a year early and moving to New York in 1976. Over the next several years, Daniels played in many different productions, including *The Farm, Minnesota Moon* and *My Life* with Christopher Reeves and William Hurt, and a one-man show, *Johnny Got His Gun*, for which he won a 1983 Obie Award. Daniels' television appearances include *Invasion of Privacy, A Rumor of War, The Visit, The Jackie Presser Story* and *No Place Like Home*. A listing of some of Daniels' film credits includes: *Ragtime, Terms of Endearment, The Purple Rose of Cairo, Heartburn, Marie, Something Wild, Radio Days, House on Carroll Street, Checking Out, Welcome Back Roxy Carmichael, The Butcher's Wife, Grand Tour, Arachnophobia, Gettysburg, Speed, Dumb & Dumber, Fly Away Home, 2 Days in the Valley, 101 Dalmatians, Trial And Error, Pleasantville, My Favorite Martian* and *All The Rage*. Daniels established the Purple Rose Theatre Company in Chelsea, Michigan, featuring midwestern actors, directors, playwrights and designers. He has written several plays, including *Shoe Man, The Tropical Pickle, The Vast Difference, Thy Kingdom's Coming, Apartment 3A* and *Boom Town*. Daniels also formed a Michigan-based film production company; an independent film of his screenplay *Escanaba In Da Moonlight* will be shot on location in the spring of 2000.

Dr. Mat Dawson, Jr. is a 77-year-old skilled tradesman who started working for Ford Motor Company in 1940 and still works there today. By investing his money, he has given away more than $1,000,000 to charitable causes. He started the Mat Dawson Jr. Endowed Scholarship at Wayne State University, which provides full tuition for four years and is open to all students, regardless of race, gender or religion. In 1996, Wayne State University awarded him an honorary Doctorate degree. Other recipients of his philanthropy include the United Negro College Fund, Louisiana State University, the NAACP, various churches, family and friends. Dawson also established a scholarship for $200,000 in the name of his mother, father and himself at Louisiana State University in Shreveport, LA.

David DiChiera is the founding general director of Michigan Opera Theatre in Detroit and the founding general director (1986–1996) of Opera Pacific in Orange County, California. Both are among the top 15 professional opera companies in the United States. 35 years ago, the University of California, Los Angeles graduate and former Fulbright Scholar began building regional support for opera. His highly acclaimed Overture to Opera series brought staged opera to hundreds of Michigan schools and community centers. He founded Michigan Opera Theatre in 1971 and the Music Hall Center for the Performing Arts two years later. Today, Michigan Opera Theatre is nationally recognized for its broad and innovative repertoire. Due in large part to Dr. DiChiera's charismatic leadership and resourcefulness, the recently opened Detroit Opera House has become an anchor for the city's thriving theater district.

Sonny Eliot began his career at WWJ-TV, now WDIV, after World War II. He spent 33 years there, hosting a variety of programs including the 17-year series *At The Zoo* and Hudson's perennial *Thanksgiving Day Parade*. He earned his greatest reputation as a weathercaster on both Channels 4 and 2. His witty reports have been named the nation's best by the National Association of TV Program Executives (NATPE). He has also received the Sloan Award for his traffic safety tips at WDIV

and citations by the American Legion and American Meteorological Society. He is currently heard on WWJ Newsradio 950 and resides in Farmington Hills with his wife, Annette.

William Clay Ford, Jr. received his Bachelor of Arts degree from Princeton University and his Master's degree in Management from MIT. The great-grandson of Ford founder, Henry Ford, William Clay Ford, Jr. began working for Ford in 1979 before spending a year as an MIT fellow in 1983. He returned to Ford and served in many roles, including head of commercial vehicle marketing for Europe, Chairman of Ford Switzerland, head of Automotive Group's business strategy, head of Ford Automotive Commercial Truck Vehicle Center and Chairman of the Finance Committee before being named Chairman of Ford Motor Company. He is also Vice Chairman of the Detroit Lions.

Stewart Francke grew up in Saginaw, Michigan, where his father was the mayor for much of the sixties. It was a time and place of industriousness, security, racial conflict and untended hope. Francke left Saginaw at 17; by age 20 he was playing in blues bands and landing gigs playing bass with the likes of Chuck Berry, Luther Allison and Jerry Lee Lewis. His hit single, *Kiss Kiss Bang Bang* was used as an episode theme for the popular TV show *Melrose Place*. Francke has also placed songs on *The Young and The Restless* and *Another World*. A nationally recognized music writer, Francke has written many articles on musicians and pop culture. His writing has appeared in Detroit's *Metro Times, CD Review, The Boston Phoenix, The Detroit News* and *The Minneapolis City Pages*. Francke lives in the metropolitan Detroit area with his wife, Julia, and their two children.

Marshall Fredericks taught at Cranbrook Academy of Art and Cranbrook and Kingswood Schools in Bloomfield Hills, Michigan from 1932 until he enlisted in the armed forces in 1942. After World War II, he worked on his numerous commissions for fountains, memorials, free-standing sculptures, reliefs, and portraits in bronze and other materials. Fredericks was the recipient of a multitude of American and foreign awards and decorations for his artistic and humanitarian achievements. He served as Royal Danish Consul for Michigan from 1965 to 1995 and worked full-time in his Royal Oak and Bloomfield Hills, Michigan studios until just days before his death April 4, 1998. The Marshall M. Fredericks Sculpture Museum in Saginaw houses original models for many of Fredricks' greatest sculptures, including *Christ on the Cross*, Indian River, Michigan; *The Fountain of Eternal Life*, Cleveland; *The Expanding Universe Fountain*, State Department, Washington, D.C.; *The Freedom of the Human Spirit*, Flushing Meadow Park, New York City; *The Leaping Gazelle* for The Levi Barbour Fountain, Belle Isle, Detroit; *The Spirit of Detroit*, City/County Building, Detroit; and *The Ford Empire and Harlequin Reliefs*, Ford Auditorium, Detroit.

Bill Frieder retired after 32 years of basketball coaching on September 10, 1997. Over the past two years he has been a basketball television analyst on Fox and a radio analyst, as well as a commercial spokesperson for Bank-One Arizona. He is also Camp Administrator for the Michael Jordan Fantasy Camp and Director of the Jason Kidd Basketball Camps and Clinics. During his coaching career, Frieder achieved many milestones. He was the second-winningest coach in Arizona State University and University of Michigan history. At Arizona State, he is credited with rebuilding the program, when he led them to postseason play for six consecutive years. Frieder coached at University of Michigan from 1981 to 1989 and led the team to back-to-back Big Ten championships in 1985 and 1986. Associated Press and Basketball Weekly named him National Coach of the Year in 1985.

Brenda Goodman was born in Detroit, Michigan on July 21, 1943. She was a student at the Center for Creative Studies, in Detroit, from 1961 to 1965. In 1976, she moved to New York and established a studio/residence in lower Manhattan, where she continues to live and work. In recent summers, she has painted in the Catskill Mountains in upstate New York. She has received grants including a National Endowment for the Arts "Visual Arts Fellowship" (1991) and a New York Foundation for the Arts "Artist Fellowship" (1994). She has taught at universities and fine arts institutes. In addition to many gallery exhibitions nationwide, her work is exhibited in permanent collections at the Detroit Institute of Arts, the John D. and Catherine T. MacArthur Foundation in Chicago, the Museum of Contemporary Art in Chicago, and the Santa Barbara Museum of Art in California. Goodman has painted continuously for 38 years.

Jennifer Granholm attended University of California at Berkley and Harvard Law School. Before becoming Michigan Attorney General in 1998, she spent four years as prosecutor for the U.S. Attorney's office, then she became head of the Wayne County Corporation Counsel's office, spearheaded the creation of a Wayne County Ethics ordinance. Granholm was also Editor in Chief of the *Harvard Civil Rights/Civil Liberties Law Review.*

Tyree Guyton grew up in Detroit and wanted to be an artist from the age of nine. In 1986, he began the controversial Heidelberg Project, which, through colorful paint and found objects, transformed a street of abandoned lots and houses into controversial artscape. This work has become internationally known and has become the third-largest tourist attraction in the city of Detroit. His work has earned him an appearance on the *Oprah Winfrey Show,* countless awards, international publicity and a 30-minute documentary licensed by HBO.

Julie Harris has received five Tony Awards, the most ever won by a performer. She received them for her portrayal of Sally Bowles in *I Am a Camera* in 1952, as St. Joan in *The Lark* in 1956, for *Forty Carats* in 1969, for *The Last Mrs. Lincoln,* and in 1977, she won the unprecedented fifth Tony as Emily Dickinson in *The Belle of Amherst.* Harris also received five additional nominations for *The Au Pair Man, Marathon '33, Skyscraper, Lucifer's Child* and *The Gin Game.* On film, Harris was nominated for an Academy Award as Frankie in *The Member of the Wedding.* Her other films include *East of Eden, The Truth About Women, Requiem for a Heavyweight, Harper, The People Next Door, Reflections in a Golden Eye, The Hiding Place, The Dark Half, Housesitter* and *The First of May.* Her TV appearances have garnered her two Emmy awards for *Little Moon of Alban* and *Victoria Regina.* Harris also portrayed Lillimae Clements on the series *Knots Landing.*

Ernie Harwell is known as Detroit's "voice of summer;" he began broadcasting baseball in 1948 and has been the Tigers' radio broadcaster since 1960. In his 52 years of broadcasting, he has only missed two games. Harwell began sportswriting at the age of 16 for the *Sporting News* and the *Atlanta Constitution;* in 1940 he became a radio sportscaster. He served four years in the Marine Corps, then from 1948 to 1950 he broadcast televised baseball with the Brooklyn Dodgers, then broadcast the Giants for four years and the Orioles for six years. In 1981 he became the first active broadcast announcer to be inducted into the Baseball Hall of Fame.

John Lee Hooker was born in Clarksdale, Mississippi. He migrated to Detroit in the mid-1930s, where he developed his music working the city's bars and nightclubs. Among Hooker's first recordings in 1948, *Boogie Chillen* became his first million-seller. This was soon followed by an even bigger hit, *I'm In The Mood.* Another surge in Hooker's career took place with the release of more than 100 songs on Vee Jay Records during the 1950s and 1960s. Young British artists such as the Animals and the Yardbirds introduced Hooker's sound to new and eager audiences, and he reached superstar status in England during the mid 1960s. By 1970, he had moved to California and worked on several projects with rock musicians including Van Morrison. He appeared in the Blues Brothers movie, which heightened his profile further. In 1989, his album *The Healer* received critical acclaim and sales in excess of a million copies. His influence on younger generations has been documented on television with features on Showtime and a special edition of the BBC's *Late Show* as well as appearances on shows including *The Tonight Show* and *Late Night with David Letterman.* In 1990 musical greats paid tribute to him with a performance in Madison Square Garden. He was inducted into the Rock 'n' Roll Hall Of Fame in 1991 and Los Angeles' Rock Walk, and in 1997 was given a star in the Hollywood Walk of Fame. At the age of 80, Hooker received his third and fourth Grammy Awards, for Best Traditional Blues Recording *(Don't Look Back)* and for Best Pop Collaboration for the song *Don't Look Back,* which he recorded with Van Morrison. Widely recognized for his "boogie" guitar style, he has influenced an entire generation of blues musicians and remains one of the most prominent blues artists alive today.

Gordie Howe, to literally millions of sports fans worldwide, is Mr. Hockey.® With one of the most illustrious careers and distinguished records in the history of any professional sport, Howe began his career at the age of 16 with the Detroit Red Wings, and spent 26 years in the NHL, 25 of those as #9 with the Red Wings. In 1973, Howe made an unprecedented return to the ice after setting 11 NHL records in Detroit (including 7 MVP awards in the NHL and WHA, the All Time Scoring Record, first 50-year-old to play major league hockey, etc.) Howe came out of retirement to play for the Houston Aeros of the WHA becoming, when sons Mark and Marty also signed with the team, the first and only father and sons combination in a major professional sport. Howe has been called the greatest all-around player of all time.

Colleen Howe, known as Mrs. Hockey,® is a future hall-of-famer, a legendary builder of youth hockey programs and the first woman manager in all of professional sports. She negotiated the first multi-player, multi-year contract in hockey and built Michigan's first indoor hockey rink. Colleen and Gordie have four children and nine grandchildren and offer much of the proceeds from their books to charitable causes.

Denise Ilitch is Vice Chairwoman of Little Caesar Enterprises, Inc.; president of Olympia Development (a Detroit real estate and entertainment development company) and Executive Vice President of Ilitch Ventures, Inc., a privately held Michigan corporation that manages the Ilitch family's Little Caesar Enterprises, Olympia Entertainment, Olympia Development, the Detroit Tigers, the Detroit Red Wings, the Detroit Rockers and Olympia Specialty Foods. She was inducted into Detroit's International Heritage Hall of Fame in 1999.

Neeme Järvi was born on June 7, 1937 in Tallinn, Estonia; Neeme Järvi is one of the world's most recorded conductors, with over 300 titles in his discography. He has been internationally acclaimed for his performances with orchestras and opera houses around the world. Mr. Järvi is also an acknowledged leader in the crusade to resuscitate neglected works by both popular and lesser-known composers. Since coming to Detroit in 1990, Järvi's exceptional artistry has garnered international attention through acclaimed performances, at home and abroad, recordings and radio broadcasts.

Al Kaline played for the Detroit Tigers from 1953 through 1974. In 1980, he became just the 10th player ever elected to the Baseball Hall of Fame in his first year of eligibility. He was selected to 18 All-Star Games over his career, including 15 out of 16 between 1955 and 1967. He posted 399 career home runs while maintaining a .297 lifetime batting average. Kaline was the first Tiger to have his number retired, and he has spent every year since 1976 in the Tiger television broadcast booth.

Peter Karmanos, Jr. is Chairman of the Board of Directors, Chief Executive Officer and co-founder of Compuware Corporation. He also co-owns three hockey teams: the Carolina Hurricanes, the Plymouth Whalers and the Florida Everglades. In memory of his late wife, Karmanos established the Barbara Ann Karmanos Cancer Institute. Now remarried to wife Debra, both are devoted to philanthropic causes and, in 1995, co-chaired the first major fundraiser for HAVEN, a shelter for victims of domestic violence. Karmanos has received many awards, including the Gerald R. Ford Sportsperson of the Year award from the Michigan Sports Hall of Fame and the prestigious Lester Patrick Trophy for his work with youth hockey programs. The proud father of three sons, Peter Karmanos, Jr. and Debra live in metropolitan Detroit.

David Patrick Kelly was born in Detroit in 1951 and graduated with a BFA Cum Laude from the University of Detroit. He has appeared in 18 feature films including *Warriors, 48HRS, Last Man Standing, Flirting With Disaster, The Crow, Crooklyn, Dreamscape, In Too Deep* and *Wild At Heart*. He also played Jerry Horne on the television series *Twin Peaks*. Mr. Kelly has appeared on Broadway in the musical *Working*, Gogol's *The Government Inspector*, and in Shakespeare's *Twelfth Night*. In 1998 he received an OBIE award for Sustained Excellence.

Judge Cornelia G. Kennedy graduated from the University of Michigan with an A.B. Degree in 1945 and a J.D. degree with distinction in 1947. She practiced law with her father, Elmer H. Groefsema, and later with her sister, Margaret C. Schaeffer, before becoming a partner in the Detroit law firm of Markle and Markle. She was elected to the Third Judicial Circuit, Wayne County, Michigan in 1966 and was appointed to the United States District Court for the Eastern District of Michigan in 1970 and was Chief Judge from 1977–1979. She was appointed to the United States Court of Appeals for the Sixth Circuit in 1979 by President Jimmy Carter and serves there today. Judge Kennedy has also held numerous positions of leadership in professional organizations, including being a director of the Detroit Bar Association, a founding member of the National Association of Women Judges, and a member of the Executive Committee of the Judicial Administration Division for the American Bar Association.

Christine Lahti was born in Birmingham, Michigan, and wanted to act from an early age. At University of Michigan she majored in language, speech and drama. In 1978, she received a Theatre World Award for her performance in the play, *The Woods*. She received a 1984 New York Film Critics Award for Best Supporting Actress and Oscar nomination for Supporting Actress in *Swing Shift* and a 1988 Los Angeles Film Critics Circle Award for Best Actress in *Running On Empty*. Her other films include *Housekeeping* and *And Justice for All* with Al Pacino and *Whose Life Is It Anyway* with Richard Dreyfus. In 1995, she received an Oscar for Best Director of a live-action short film, *Lieberman in Love*. Lahti also portrayed Dr. Kate Austin in television's medical drama, *Chicago Hope*, work for which she received a Golden Globe and an Emmy Award in 1998. Lahti lives in California with her husband, director Thomas Schlamme, and three children.

Elmore Leonard became interested in writing around 1935, after reading a serialization of *All Quiet on the Western Front* in the *Detroit Times*. After graduating from high school, he served in the Navy until 1946, when he enrolled in the University of Detroit. He graduated in 1950 with a major in English and Philosophy. In 1949, while still in college, he joined Campbell-Ewald Advertising, and by 1953 he published his first novel, *The Bounty Hunters*. Leonard has written 35 novels, including bestsellers such as *Cuba Libre, Out of Sight, Rum Punch, Get Shorty, Maximum Bob, Pronto, Riding the Rap, Glitz, Freaky Deaky,* and *Killshot*. Three of his books *(The Switch, Split Images* and *LaBrava)* have been nominated for the Edgar Allan Poe Award by the Mystery Writers of America. His novel *Maximum Bob* was awarded the first annual International Association of Crime Writers' North American Hammett Prize in 1991. In 1992, the Mystery Writers gave Leonard the Grand Master Award. His books *Get Shorty, Out of Sight* and *Rum Punch* have been made into movies; many more are in production. He has also written numerous screenplays. A full-length biography, *Elmore Leonard*, was published by Continuum as part of their Literature and Life series, and a documentary entitled *Elmore Leonard's Criminal Record*, produced in 1991 by the BBC, aired on The Learning Channel. Leonard lives in Bloomfield Hills, Michigan.

Philip Levine was born in Detroit, Michigan, in 1928. He is the author of sixteen books of poetry, most recently *The Mercy*, published by Alfred A. Knopf. His other poetry collections include *The Simple Truth* (Alfred A. Knopf, 1994), which won the Pulitzer Prize; *What Work Is* (1991), which won the National Book Award; *New Selected Poems* (1991); *Ashes: Poems New and Old* (1979), which received the National Book Critics Circle Award and the first American Book Award for Poetry; *7 Years From Somewhere* (1979), which won the National Book Critics Circle Award; and *The Names of the Lost* (1975), which won the Lenore Marshall Poetry

Prize. He has also published a collection of essays, *The Bread of Time: Toward an Autobiography* (1994), edited *The Essential Keats* (1987), and co-edited and translated two books: *Off the Map: Selected Poems of Gloria Fuertes* (with Ada Long, 1984) and *Tarumba: The Selected Poems of Jaime Sabines* (with Ernesto Trejo, 1979). He has received the Ruth Lilly Poetry Prize, the Harriet Monroe Memorial Prize from Poetry, the Frank O'Hara Prize, and two Guggenheim Foundation fellowships. For two years he served as chair of the Literature Panel of the National Endowment for the Arts. He lives in New York City and Fresno, California, and teaches at New York University.

Maurice Lezell, known to most Detroiters as "Mr. Belvedere," was born in Kentucky; his family moved to Detroit when he was three years old. He served in the Coast Guard for three and a half years during World War II, then returned home and began doing home remodeling work. He named his company Belvedere Construction. The company grew to become one of the largest remodeling firms and local advertisers in Detroit. During the '70s and '80s, Lezell appeared in television segments with Bill Kennedy and Conrad Patrick. He worked to raise money for charities such as March of Dimes and used his advertising to raise interest in local events such as the Michigan State Fair. Belvedere Construction is now 51 years old; Lezell is semi-retired.

Jerry Linenger was born and raised in Eastpointe and graduated from East Detroit High School. A retired U.S. Navy Captain and flight surgeon, he holds two doctorates (an MD and Ph.D.), two master's degrees, as well as three Honorary Doctorates (Wayne State University, Michigan Tech and Northern Michigan University). Linenger spent five months in space aboard the space station Mir, where he logged 50 million miles and fought the most severe fire to occur in space. He was the first American to undock from the Mir space station in a Russian Soyuz capsule and was the first American to do a spacewalk in a Russian spacesuit. At the time, he also set the record for the longest time for an American male in space: 132 days, four hours and one minute. He now runs Linenger Communications, is the author of *Off The Planet* (McGraw-Hill, 2000, 1-800-450-8618) and does motivational speaking via Washington Speakers Bureau in Alexandria, Virginia. Linenger lives in Northern Michigan with his wife and three sons.

Ed Love has earned a national reputation for his knowledge of and respect for jazz. His radio career stretches back to Armed Forces Radio in the Philippines in the early '50s. He worked at a station in Independence, Kansas, near his hometown, and later worked in Beckley, West Virginia and Baltimore, Maryland before coming to Detroit and sister stations WCHB-AM and WCHD (now WCHB) FM. In addition to his radio work, which took him to WJLB-AM and WQRS-FM prior to WDET, Love was a booth announcer at WXYZ-TV (Channel 7) and host of a jazz TV interview series on Detroit cable. In the 1960s, he co-founded a series of weekly jazz workshops with LeBaron Taylor that helped develop such budding Detroit music talents as pianist Kirk Lightsey and saxophonist Bennie Maupin. He hosted *Evolution of Jazz,* which aired on more than 125 stations coast to coast from 1988 to 1994. Ed Love can be heard on WDET, 101.9 FM, weekdays from 7:00 to 10:00 PM; the year 2000 will mark his 18th year at WDET.

Adam Cardinal Maida was ordained a priest May 26, 1956, by the then Bishop John Dearden of the Diocese of Pittsburgh. Following his ordination, he served in the Pittsburgh Diocese, most notably as Vice Chancellor and General Counsel. On November 7, 1983, Fr. Maida was appointed the ninth Bishop of Green Bay and was ordained bishop on January 25, 1984. Bishop Maida was appointed to various Papal Commissions concerning legal matters and served as a member of several national church committees and organizations dealing with canonical law. Bishop Maida was installed as Archbishop of Detroit on June 12, 1990, and elevated to the College of Cardinals by Pope John Paul II on November 26, 1994. As Archbishop of Detroit, Cardinal Maida has been instrumental in the founding of the Cornerstone Schools, the Religious Leaders Forum, Partners in Service, St. John's Center for Youth and Family, Project Life, an archdiocesan endowment, Jubilee 2000, and the Pope John Paul II Cultural Center in Washington, DC.

Sue Marx is an Academy Award-winning filmmaker and president of Sue Marx Films, Inc. and Urban Communications Group. Since forming her company in 1980, Marx has produced and directed over 150 promotional, corporate, political and educational films and videos, and numerous radio and TV spots. Her work has been seen on PBS, BBC, CBC, Bravo, The Movie Channel, Arts & Entertainment and The Learning Channel, and has been broadcast around the world. The United States Information Agency (USIA) has acquired several titles, and many are in libraries, museums and educational institutions around the world. In 1988, Marx received an Academy Award for *Young At Heart,* which screened at the New York Film Festival and the Telluride Film Festival. She has also won 16 Emmys, several CINE Golden Eagles and top awards from the New York Festivals. Prior to starting her own company, Marx was a photographic model, worked in public relations, was a freelance photojournalist, and for eight years, wrote and produced the award-winning documentary series, *Profiles in Black,* at Channel 4. She received her graduate degree from Wayne State University, is married, has three daughters and lives in Detroit.

Ann Mikolowski grew up on Detroit's East Side and attended the Society for Arts and Crafts (now Center for Creative Studies) and Wayne State University. In 1969, together with her husband, Ken Mikolowski, she started *The Alternative Press,* which received a National Endowment for the Arts award in 1974 and which her husband still publishes today. Ann's artwork has won two Creative Artist awards from Michigan Council for the Arts. She has exhibited solo shows in New York, San Francisco and Detroit and Ann Arbor galleries. Her work is also in the permanent collection of the Detroit Institute of Arts as well as numerous public collections, private collections, and corporate collections including MichCon, WDIV and Absolut Vodka. Ann passed away in August 1999.

Ken Mikolowski grew up in Detroit's Cass Corridor area and majored in English at Wayne State University, where he began writing poetry and was founding editor of the Wayne Review, a literary magazine. He graduated in 1964. In 1969, Mikolowski and his wife, Ann, started *The Alternative Press,* a publication which received a National Endowment for the Arts award in 1974 and which he still publishes today. He has published three books of poetry: *Thank You Call Again, little mysteries,* and *Big Enigmas.* Mikolowski teaches creative writing at the University of Michigan's Residential College and has received three Creative Artist Awards from Michigan Council for the Arts.

Shirley Muldowney, a legend in drag racing, is the most successful woman in motorsports history. Her unprecedented career has broken gender and racing barriers and become an inspiration for neophyte racers everywhere. She began racing competitively in 1958, was the first woman to be licensed by the NHRA to drive a top fuel dragster, the only woman to have won a professional category in the Winston World Championship and was the first driver ever to repeat as the World Champion. Including her AHRA World Championship, Muldowney has now won four such championships. Her awards and honors include a 1977 "Outstanding Achievement Award" from the United States House of Representatives. She was named to the American Auto Racing Writers & Broadcasters Association All-American Team five times and the United States Sports Academy's Top 25 Professional female athletes from 1992–1997. The theatrical release *Heart Like a Wheel* chronicled Muldowney's life, and in 1990, she became the first woman and second drag racer to be inducted into the Motorsports Hall of Fame.

Ted Nugent is considered the world's number one guitar showman. He was born in 1948, began bowhunting in 1953 and playing guitar in 1956. He has recorded 29 albums since 1967 and has sold over 30 million albums worldwide. He hosts the *Ted Nugent Morning Show* on WWBR radio in Detroit, and is the creator and host of Detroit's *Ted Nugent Commando Radio* show which has aired for the past 10 years. He is the editor and publisher of *Adventure Outdoors Magazine,* the president of Ted Nugent United Sportsmen of America, the founder of Ted Nugent Kamp for Kids and Ted Nugent Bowhunting School, and is the author of *BloodTrails: The Truth About Bowhunting.* His award-winning *Ted Nugent Spirit of the Wild* PBS video series raised more than $3,000,000 for PBS affiliates natinonwide. He has been outspoken against drugs and alcohol throughout his career.

Harvey Ovshinsky is president of HKO Media, Inc., a film and video production company. *The Detroit News* has described Ovshinsky as one of this country's finest storytellers. His documentaries have been awarded a national Emmy, a Peabody award, an Alfred I. DuPont–Columbia University Awards Silver Baton, and the American Film Institute's Robert M. Bennett Award for Excellence. Before starting HKO Media, Ovshinsky was a producer at WDIV-TV and WXYZ-TV and Director of Production at WTVS-TV. He was the original editor and publisher of Detroit's underground newspaper, *The Fifth Estate.* Harvey was news director at WABX-FM and wrote commentaries and hosted talk shows heard on WRIF-FM, WCSX-FM and WDET-FM. He teaches screenwriting at Wayne State University and hosts writing workshops at the Community House in Birmingham and the Grosse Pointe War Memorial. Harvey is also on the faculty of the Grosse Pointe Academy, where he teaches creative writing to students in the 4th through 8th grade.

Stan Ovshinsky founded Energy Conversion Devices (ECD) with his wife, Dr. Iris M. Ovshinsky, in order to continue his pioneering work in amorphous and disordered materials, a field he began in 1955. He is also CEO of Ovonic Battery Company, president and CEO of United Solar (a joint venture with Canon), and chairman of the Institute for Amorphous Studies. His work in information storage and control includes optical and electrical memories, switching, three-dimensional intelligent computers and amorphous integrated circuits. He has many

basic patents and well over 200 U.S. patents. In 1968 he received the Diesel Gold Medal for Invention presented by the German Inventors Association. He was awarded a Doctor of Science degree from Lawrence Technological University and honorary Doctor of Engineering degree from Bowling Green State University and an honorary Doctorate of Science from Jordan College and is an adjunct professor of Engineering. at Wayne State University. In 1987 Ovshinsky was profiled for one hour on the public television science series *NOVA*. In 1988 he received the Coors American Ingenuity Award, and he received the Toyota Award for Advancement in 1991. In 1993 he was named Corporate Detroiter of the Year. *Time Magazine* named him Hero for the Planet, he received the Karl Boer Solar energy Medal of Merit from the University of Delaware and the International Solar Energy Society, and he has been inducted into the Michigan Chemical Engineering Hall of Fame.

Dr. Jai Krishna Prasad received his Master of Surgery degree from Patna University in India in 1966. He completed eight years of post-doctoral training in the United Kingdom, then moved to London, Ontario, Canada, as chief resident in surgery at University of Ontario's Westminster Hospital in 1974 and senior resident in pathology in 1975. In 1976 he moved to University of Michigan Hospital as a burn fellow and instructor. He became co-director of its Burn Center and chief of its division of burns in 1987. He moved to Detroit Receiving Hospital in 1992 as director of the Burn Center. Dr. Prasad has lectured internationally and served as a moderator for the American Burn Association, the International Congress of Burn Injuries and the Sino-American Burn Trauma Conference. In 1997 he received the Michigan Health and Hospital Association Patric E. Ludwig Community Benefit Award for his Frostbite Prevention Program.

Heinz C. Prechter is the Chairman and Founder of ASC Incorporated in Southgate, Michigan. He began his automotive career in 1955 at age thirteen when he became an apprentice in automotive coach-building and interior trim in the city of Nuremberg, Germany. In 1963, he moved to San Francisco as an exchange student. Soon after, he founded the American Sunroof Company in a two-car garage. Today, ASC Incorporated is the flagship of a conglomerate of automotive, newspaper, real estate, and investment companies with 60 facilities and 5,300 employees worldwide and annual revenues under management exceeding $900 million. Mr. Prechter has been widely recognized for his entrepreneurial accomplishments, broad community involvement and political achievements. He serves as board member of various global businesses and was Chairman of the President's Export Council during President Bush's administration.

Elizabeth Punsalan was born in Syracuse, NY and grew up in Ohio where she began skating at the age of seven. She and her partner on and off the ice, Jerod Swallow, teamed up in 1989. They captured their first National Championship in 1991 and married in 1993. Revered as the country's most creative and exciting ice dance team, their career achievements include five U.S. National Championship titles, a Skate America crown, a U.S. Olympic Festival Championship title, silver medal honors in Trophy Lalique and the U.S. Pro-Am Challenge, as well as 34 medals in national and international competitions.

Dick Purtan earned his reputation as Detroit's most respected and recognized air personality through many years of hard work, dedication and immense talent. As host of the Oldies 104.3 WOMC *Morning Show* with Purtan's People, he entertains his loyal following with comedic commentary and topical wit. Prior to WOMC, Purtan hosted shows on WXYZ Radio (now WXYT) CKLW, WCZY, WKQI and WKNR (Keener 13), where he started in Detroit in 1965. He has twice been named *Billboard Magazine*'s Major Market Air Personality of the Year and was voted Best Air Personality at the 1986 International Radio Festival in New York. In 1993, Purtan won the "Oscar of Radio," the National Association of Broadcasters MARCONI Award as Major Market Air Personality of the Year and recently won the 1999 Air Personality of the Year award from *Radio and Records,* the industry trade journal. Locally, he has received the Motor City Music Awards Radio Personality of the Year several times and was named the *Metro Times* Radio Personality of the Year five times in a row. He serves on the board of the Children's Hospital of Michigan, and his annual Salvation Army Radiothon has raised over $3.5 million for Detroit's hungry and homeless over the last 12 years. Purtan and his wife, Gail, have six daughters.

Gregory J. Reed, a graduate of Michigan State University and Wayne State University, is an attorney in the areas of entertainment, sports and corporate law; he has represented Anita Baker, Johnnie Cochrane, Jr., the Winans, Wynton Marsalis and the Four Tops. He is the author of *Economic Empowerment Through the Church: A Blueprint for Progressive Community Development,* which received the American Book Award. He also co-authored *Quiet Strength* with Rosa Parks, a book that appeared on 20 best-seller lists. In this century's largest acquisition in African-American literary history, he purchased *The Autobiography of Malcolm X* from the estate of Alex Haley. He is the founder of the Gregory J. Reed Scholarship Foundation, which aids students in arts, engineering and law, and he is the co-founder of The Parks Legacy to preserve Rosa Parks papers and archives. Reed has been honored with citations in a number of Who's Who compilations, including Entertainment, Black Americans, American Lawyers and Finance. He was also inducted into the Hall of Fame of Entertainment Law.

Martha Reeves was born in Eufala, Alabama and moved to Detroit before she was a year old. In her teens, she was discovered by Hitsville USA. Along with her powerful backup group, the Vandellas, Martha Reeves created some of the most memorable rhythm and blues chartbuster records of the 1960s, including *Heat Wave* (1961), *Dancing In The Streets* (1964), *Nowhere To Run* (1965) and *Jimmy Mack* (1967). Martha Reeves later embarked on a solo career, signing with MCA Records in 1973 and later with Arista Records in 1977. In 1995, she was inducted into the Alabama Music Hall of Fame. She still performs live throughout the world today and works with many local and national charity organizations.

Rabbi Charles H. Rosenzveig was born in Poland and immigrated to the United States in 1947. He attended Yeshiva University, where he was ordained as a Rabbi in 1949. He married and moved to Detroit in 1951, where he served as Rabbi of Congregation Mount Sinai in Port Huron until 1993. He was also Professor of Rabbinics at the Midrasha, College of Jewish Studies in Southfield until 1984. In 1981, he founded the Holocaust Memorial Center, where he currently serves as Executive

Vice President. He was Adjunct Professor of Jewish History at University of Detroit in 1990. He was Project Director of *The World Reacts to the Holocaust,* published by John Hopkins University Press in 1966. He received the Michiganian of the Year Award in 1994 and was inducted into Detroit s International Institute Hall of Fame in 1966.

Mitch Ryder and his band, the Detroit Wheels, served as the musical bridge between the Motown soul factory and the high-energy, take-no-prisoners rock'n'roll that would roar out of Detroit via Iggy & The Stooges, the MC5, Ted Nugent and Bob Seger. Born William Levise, Jr., Ryder was performing as Billy Lee in a high school band called Tempest. In 1964, he encountered a group that included Jim McCarty, Earl Elliot and John Badanjek. Together with rhythm guitarist Joe Kubert, they formed Billy Lee & The Rivieras. After succeeding in live local performances, the group moved to New York in 1965 and their explosive songs hit the charts, including *Jenny Take A Ride, Little Latin Lupe Lu, Shake A Tail Feather,* and their *Devil With A Blue Dress On* and *Good Golly Miss Molly* medley, which hit #4 in 1966. Early in 1967, Ryder recorded *The Detroit-Memphis Experiment* album with Booker T. & The MGs and the Memphis Horns. Ryder returned to Detroit in 1971, later moved to Denver where he honed his songwriting skills for five years, then returned to Detroit where he has released several new albums, including *Red Blood, White Mink* and *In The China Shop.*

Soupy Sales grew up in Huntington, West Virginia. After receiving his B.A. in Journalism at Marshall University, he landed a job as a radio writer at a station in Huntington and later went on the air to become the area's top-rated DJ. He moved to Cincinnati in 1950 and began working in television, and *Soupy's Soda Shop* became America's first teenage dance TV program. Sales moved to Cleveland in 1951, then to Detroit in 1953 and quickly became the Motor City's top-rated TV personality. He helmed 11 hours of TV time each week, including *Lunch With Soupy Sales,* the first non-cartoon Saturday morning program on the ABC-TV network. His format became an inspiration for many children's shows to come. He moved to the West Coast in 1960, and his *Soupy Sales Show* became L.A.'s number-one show. In 1964, Sales took his show to New York. The show was soon seen throughout the U.S. and Canada, Australia and New Zealand. Sales appeared on the prime-time shows of Ed Sullivan, Dean Martin, Bob Hope and Carol Burnett. In 1968 he joined the panel of *What's My Line?* and in 1978 co-starred on *Sha Na Na.* In the '80s, Sales gave SRO nightclub performances, appeared on panel shows and was a semi-regular on *TV's Bloopers and Practical Jokes.* Sales continues to give live performances and appear at speaking engagements.

Norbert Schemansky has been called the greatest weightlifter of all time. After serving in World War II (he is a decorated veteran), Schemansky received the Silver medal in heavyweight weightlifting in the 1948 Summer Olympic Games. He took the Gold medal in the 1952 Olympic Games, and then the Bronze in 1960 and 1964. During his Olympic career, he set 27 world records. Schemansky also won the World Championship title in 1951, 1953 and 1954, won the gold medal in weightlifting in the 1955 Pan-American Games and is a nine-time National Champion. Schemansky is also listed in the 1994 Guinness Book of World Records as the oldest lifter to win an Olympic medal (in 1964 at the age of 40) and as the only lifter to four separate Olympic Games.

Bo Schembechler, former Miami (Ohio) and Michigan Head Coach, is winningest coach in Michigan football history. The Barberton, Ohio native played college football at Miami (Ohio), graduated in 1951, and received his master's degree in 1952 from Ohio State, where he served as a graduate assistant coach. After serving in the U.S. Army, Schembechler became assistant coach at Presbyterian College (1954) and Bowling Green (1955). He then joined Ara Parseghian's staff at Northwestern in 1958 before spending the next five seasons as assistant to Woody Hayes at Ohio State. In 1963 he was appointed head coach at Miami (Ohio). In 1969, he began coaching at the University of Michigan, where 13 of his 21 Michigan teams won or tied for the Big Ten Championship and 17 went to bowl games and a top 10 national ranking. Schembechler was also the athletic director at Michigan from 1988–1991. In 1999 he was selected as the recipient of the Amos Alonzo Stagg Award presented by the American Football Coaches Association.

Jimmy Schmidt opened his first Rattlesnake Club in Denver, Colorado in 1985. Since then he has opened a second Rattlesnake in Detroit and three other restaurants in the Detroit area (Chianti Tuscan Grill, Jimmy's and Smitty's). He has released three cookbooks, *Cooking for All Seasons, Jimmy Schmidt's Cooking Class* and *Heart Healthy Cooking for All Seasons.* Schmidt is one of the co-founders of Chefs Collaborative 2000 and is now a member of the Board of Overseers, working with fellow culinary stars Jacques Pepin, Wolfgang Puck and Mark Miller to promote "personal health, the vitality of cultures, and the integrity of the global environment." The group produces educational videos and advocates seasonal and local cuisine in restaurants. Schmidt was also the 1993 recipient of the prestigious James Beard Award for Best Chef of the Midwest, and he and his restaurants have received numerous awards and accolades from publications including *Food & Wine, Esquire, Wine Spectator* and *Bon Appetit.*

Joe Schmidt grew up in Pittsburgh, Pennsylvania. He attended University of Pittsburgh and played football there from 1950 to 1953. In 1952 he was named to Associated Press and United Press All American Teams. He received his B.S. Degree in Education in 1953. He was drafted by the Detroit Lions in 1953 and was a member of the Detroit Lions 1953–1957 World Championship teams. He was voted Lions MVP four times (1955, 1957, 1958 and 1961), and he was Team Captain for nine years. Schmidt played in ten straight Pro Bowls, was elected to All NFL Pro Teams nine times, and was voted NFL MVP by Associated Press in 1960. In 1973, he was elected to the NFL Hall of Fame; he was also elected to the Pennsylvania Sports Hall of Fame, the Pittsburgh Sports Hall of Fame and the Michigan Sports Hall of Fame. After 13 years a Detroit Lions player, Schmidt retired following the 1965 season and became Linebacker Coach for the 1966 season. He served as Head Coach from 1967 to 1972, when he retired with a 43-34-7 record. He established Joe Schmidt Sales in 1973, an agency which sells to Big Three and Tier One automotive suppliers. Schmidt has five children and lives with his wife, Marilynn, in Bloomfield Hills.

Thom Sharp grew up in the ultra-liberal bastion of Dearborn. He attended Henry Ford Community College, Eastern Michigan University and went to graduate school at Wayne State University. He worked in the advertising business for nine years as a copywriter and group supervisor at Ross Roy, Yaffe Stone August and W. B. Doner. In 1975, Thom began appearing on Dick Purtan's radio show at WXYZ. This was the boost he needed. Thom left Detroit in 1977 for BBDO Advertising in Los Angeles and did stand-up comedy by night, which helped him win roles on TV shows. For the past 20 years Sharp has performed in many television and radio commercials. He has also played on numerous television shows including the *Tonight Show* and *Late Night with David Letterman,* and he guest starred as Tim Allen's older brother on *Home Improvement.* Thom is married to Judy, his college sweetheart from Henry Ford Community College; they reside in LA with their golden retriever, Bailey.

Neal Shine is the retired publisher of *The Detroit Free Press* and currently a professor of journalism at Oakland University. He was born in Detroit in 1930, grew up on the city's lower east side and still lives on the east side, a few miles from his old neighborhood.

Emanuel Steward is a Detroit-based manager and trainer who guided some of the great boxers of the '80s and '90s to world championships, including Thomas Hearns, Leon Spinks, Lennox Lewis and Evander Holyfield. He has also developed four Olympic gold medal winners. Steward began boxing in the Detroit Parks and Recreation programs. He won numerous junior and local amateur titles before winning the 1963 National Golden Gloves title in the Tournament of Champions in Chicago, leading Detroit to its first team title in 20 years. He has transformed the Kronk gym in Detroit from a neighborhood recreation center into the most famous boxing gym in the world. In the '80s, the Boxing Writers Association of America selected him twice as Manager of the Year and three times as Trainer of the Year. In 1996 he was inducted into the International Boxing Hall of Fame.

Jerod Swallow was born in Ann Arbor, Michigan and grew up in Northville. He began skating at the age of ten. He was the nation's Junior Champion in dance and ranked second in pairs in 1985. He and his partner and wife, Elizabeth Punsalan, teamed up in 1989. They captured their first National Championship in 1991 and married in 1993. Considered the country's foremost ice dance team, Swallow's and Punsalan's career includes five U.S. National Championship titles, a Skate America crown, a U.S. Olympic Festival Championship title, silver medal honors in Trophy Lalique and the U.S. Pro-Am Challenge and 34 medals in national and international competitions.

Jimmie Thompson began working for The Parade Company in 1988 as a staff artist to sculpt and paint. In the early 1990s he was promoted to Art Director, then to Vice President/Creative Director in 1999. The Parade Company produces America's Thanksgiving Day Parade as well as the Freedom Festival and many other events throughout the country and the world. Thompson's parade-related artwork has earned two Gold and one Silver award from the International Festival and Event Association, and he was 1996 Michigan Artist of the Year. In September 1999 he started his own company to expand and take his designs to the next level. His future plans include children's book illustration. He currently lives in Ferndale with his wife, Jane, an artist, and his two children, Raymond and Jennifer.

Robbie Timmons is a graduate of Ohio State University in Columbus. She began her broadcasting career in 1972 at WILX-TV in Lansing, Michigan, where she was the first woman in the country to anchor the 6 and 11 PM newscasts for a network affiliate. She moved to WJBK-TV in Detroit, where she was an anchor and reporter for six years. She married sports producer and commentator Jim Brandstatter in 1980. She then joined WXYX-TV/Channel 7 in January, 1982 and co-anchors *Action News Midday* and *Action News* at 5 p.m. She was recently honored with the prestigious Silver Circle Award in recognition of her 25 years in broadcasting. She was named Outstanding Woman in Broadcast News by the American Women in Radio and Television, and has received Emmy Awards for her reporting skills.

Lily Tomlin, one of America's foremost comediennes, has built a career spanning films, television, animation, theater and video. Born in Detroit, she enrolled at Wayne State University to study medicine before moving to New York in 1965. In 1969, she moved to California and joined the cast of *Laugh-In,* where she rose to national prominence for her characterizations as Ernestine, the telephone operator and Edith Ann, the precocious five-and-a-half year old. She went on to co-write and star in four comedy specials, *The Lily Tomlin Show* (1973), *Lily* (1973), *Lily* (1974), and *Lily Tomlin* (1975), for which she won three Emmys and a Writers Guild of America Award. Her comedy recording, *This Is A Recording,* won a Grammy in 1971. In 1977, Tomlin's Broadway debut, *Appearing Nitely,* written and directed by Jane Wagner, won her a special Tony Award. The team of Tomlin and Wagner went on to produce the Emmy-winning television special *Lily: Sold Out* (1981) and *Lily for President?* (1982). In 1986, she won a Tony Award, the Drama Desk Award and the Outer Critics' Circle Award for her Broadway show *The Search for Signs of Intelligent Life in the Universe.* Her films include *Nashville,* for which she received an Oscar nomination for Best Supporting Actress, 1975, *The Late Show, Moment By Moment, The Incredible Shrinking Woman, All Of Me, Big Business, Shadows and Fog, Short Cuts, The Beverly Hillbillies, Flirting With Disaster, Getting Away With Murder, Tea With Mussolini,* and *Krippendorf's Tribe.* She has guest starred in the television series the *X-Files, Homicide* and was the boss of *FYI* the last two seasons of *Murphy Brown.* Tomlin has also won an Emmy for her work in the animated children's series, *The Magic Schoolbus* and two Peabody Awards, the first for narrating and co-executive producing *The Celluloid Closet* and a second for the animated television special, *Edith Ann's Christmas: Just Say Noël,* which she executive produced.

Jerry Uelsmann received his B.F.A. degree at the Rochester Institute of Technology in 1957 and his M.S. and M.F.A. at Indiana University in 1960. He began teaching photography at the University of Florida in Gainesville in 1960. He has been graduate research professor of art at the university since 1974. Uelsmann received a Guggenheim Fellowship in 1967 and a National Endowment for the Arts Fellowship in 1972. He is a Fellow of the Royal Photographic Society of Great Britain, a founding member of the American Society for Photographic Education, and a trustee of the Friends of Photography. His work has been exhibited in more than 100 individual shows in the United States and abroad. His books include *Jerry N. Uelsmann* (Millerton, N.Y.: Aperture, 1970); *John L. Ward, The Criticism of Photography*

as Art: The Photographs of Jerry Uelsmann (Gainesville: University of Florida Press, 1970); *Jerry Uelsmann: Silver Meditations* (Dobbs Ferry, N.Y.: Morgan & Morgan, 1975); *Jerry N. Uelsmann: Photography from 1975-79* (Chicago: Columbia College, 1980); *Jerry N. Uelsmann—Twenty-five Years: A Retrospective* (Boston: New York Graphic Society, 1982); and *Uelsmann: Process and Perception* (Gainesville: University Presses of Florida,1985).

Wyland, the world's premier ocean artist, has been a pioneer in the marine art movement since 1971. Born in Detroit and a graduate of Center for Creative Studies, the painter, sculptor, muralist and writer has completed over 83 landmark murals, the Whaling Walls, throughout the U.S., Canada, Japan, Australia, Mexico and France (including one in Detroit, which he completed in October, 1997). *USA Today* said, "Wyland is a marine Michelangelo." Wyland's 20 years of diving brings to each of his works a three-dimensional quality that separates him from other artists in his genre. It is estimated that over one billion people a year encounter his art. His paintings and sculptures are collected worldwide and can be found on public walls, corporate collections, marine institutes, galleries and many private homes. He and his family own and operate a number of Wyland Galleries in Hawaii, California and Florida.

Steve Yzerman was born in 1965 in Cranbrook, British Columbia. He was drafted by the Detroit Red Wings in 1983, moving directly from junior hockey to the NHL. As a rookie in 1983-84 he was runner up for the Calder Memorial Trophy, and in 1984 he was named to the All-Rookie Team. Named captain of the Red Wings in 86-87, Yzerman is now the longest serving NHL team captain. In 1988-89, he was chosen by his peers as top performer in the league for the Lester B. Pearson Award. In 1997, Yzerman recorded points in every game of the Stanley Cup Final and led the Red Wings to a four-game sweep over the Philadelphia Flyers. It was the franchise's first Stanley Cup in 42 years. On June 16, 1998, Yzerman was again presented with the Cup; the Wings swept the Washington Capitals. He led all playoff scorers and was a unanimous choice for the Conn Smythe Trophy as playoff MVP. Yzerman has played in nine All-Star Games (1984, 1988, 1989, 1990, 1991, 1992, 1993 and 1997 and 2000). He has also represented Canada in the 1984 Canada Cup, World Championships in 1985, 1989 & 1990, the 1996 World Cup and 1998 Olympics. He was named First Team All-Star for the 1999-2000 season and received the 1999-2000 Frank J. Selke Trophy, given annually by the NHL to the league's best defensive forward.

motor city memoirs

ABOUT THE AUTHORS

John Sobczak has been a commercial photographer for nearly 20 years.
He has received numerous regional and national awards for his images
and has worked for many of the Fortune 500 companies, including
Ford Motor Company, Daimler-Chrysler, General Motors, AT&T
and IBM, as well as such publications as *Newsweek Fortune,
Entrepreneur* and *Parade*. *Motor City Memoirs* is his second book; his
first is *The Vision of Words*. He is currently working on his third book, a follow-up to
Vision, called *Wordlens*. Sobczak lives in Bloomfield Township with his wife, Jackie, and
three-year-old daughter, Alex.

Jennifer Thomas Vanadia grew up in Farmington and has worked, played
and lived in and around Detroit ever since. A freelance marketing and
advertising writer who has won local, national and international awards
for her work, she lives in Waterford with her husband, Sal, and their
daughter, Victoria Skye.

Joni M. Jones graduated from Michigan State University with a bachelor's
degree in studio art and advertising. She grew up in Saginaw where she
won local awards for her work. Today she is a Senior Art Director at
Victor Associates Advertising located in Bloomfield Hills. She lives in
Royal Oak with her husband, Chris and son, Ashton.

Lisa Clogg graduated from Michigan State University with a bachelor's
degree in studio art. Today she is an Associate Creative Director at Victor
Associates Advertising where she has won local awards for her work. She
lives in Oxford Township with her husband, Bill.

SPECIAL THANKS TO...

Neal Shine, Tim Kiska, Mayor Dennis W. Archer, Shella Howe, Del Reddy, Tom Maday, Shayne Bowman, Chris Willis, Giovanni Loria, Gray Reynolds, Neil Golightly, Mary Ann Toccalino, Richard Laskos, Susan M. Kornfield, Glyn Grand and photo assistants Tadd Naffin, Ed Mroz, Regan Patrick and Gary Duncan.

motor city memoirs

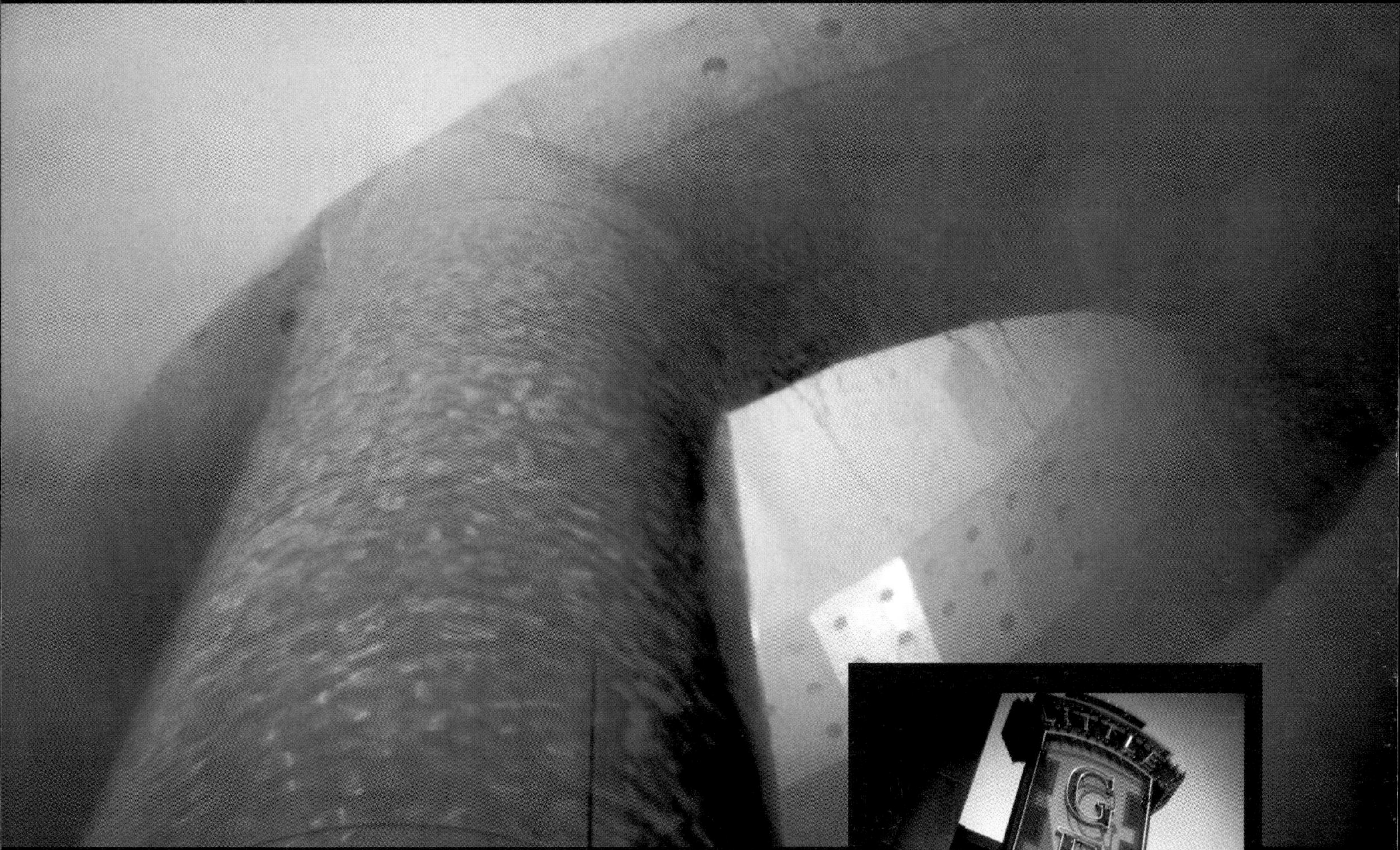

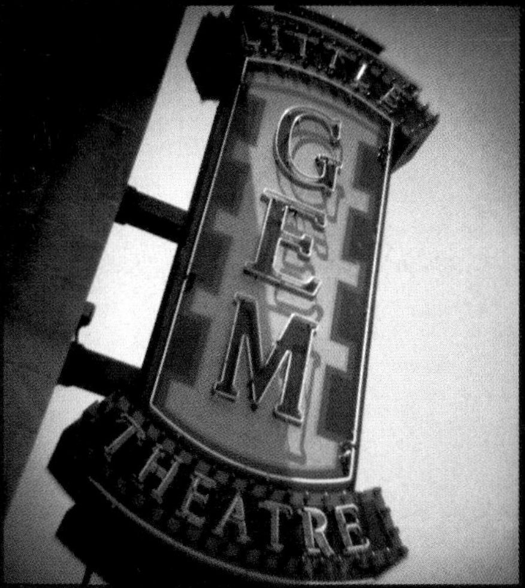
LITTLE
GEM
THEATRE